The BIG Book of
Team Building
Games

Other McGraw-Hill books by John Newstrom and Edward Scannell:

The Big Book of
Team Building
Games

Quick, Fun Activities for Building Morale, Communication and Team Spirit

John Newstrom

Edward Scannell

McGraw-Hill

New York   San Francisco   Washington, D.C.   Auckland   Bogotá
Caracas   Lisbon   London   Madrid   Mexico City   Milan
Montreal   New Delhi   San Juan   Singapore
Sydney   Tokyo   Toronto

The Big Book of Team Building Games
Quick, Fun Activities for Building Morale, Communication and Team Spirit

John Newstrom, Edward Scannell

ISBN: 0077114752

 **Professional**

Published by:
McGraw-Hill Publishing Company
Shoppenhangers Road, Maidenhead, Berkshire, England, SL6 2QL
Telephone: 44 (0) 1628 502500
Fax: 44 (0) 1628 770224
Website: www.mcgraw-hill.co.uk

British Library Cataloguing in Publication Data
A catalogue record of this book is available from the British Library.

Library of Congress Cataloging Number: 97-42110

McGraw-Hill books are available at special quantity discounts. Please contact
the corporate sales executive.

Reprinted 2007, 2008, 2009

Printed and bound in Great Britain by Bell & Bain Ltd., Glasgow

The **McGraw·Hill** Companies

Contents

**Chapter 12.   How Can We Build Self-esteem? Affirming Ourselves
through Games**   *229*

Acknowledgments

Any project like this is always a team effort. There is no way we could possibly thank the thousands of "team members" who have continually encouraged and assisted us in our continuing quest to make meetings more effective.

To the thousands of friends and colleagues who have attended our seminars and workshops for such groups as the American Society for Training and Development, Meeting Professionals, Int'l., and the National Speakers Association, we are most grateful. They have helped us field-test the items in this book and have contributed to many of its ideas.

For the continuing assistance from the McGraw-Hill team of Philip Ruppel and Richard Narramore, we are truly indebted. They have become friends as well as our publishing team.

Thank you!

John Newstrom

Edward Scannell

Introduction to Team Building Games

Organizations hire individuals, but almost all employees work in one or more *teams* (cooperative small groups engaging in regular, coordinated action to attain results). As a matter of fact, teams have become an international phenomenon, as illustrated by the popularity (and high expectations placed upon) the U.S. Olympic "Dream Teams" in basketball in recent years. And when managers in one study were asked to name the most important traits of a perfect staff member, *being a "team player" was ranked the highest,* ahead of factors such as dedication, problem solving, experience, and good communication. Clearly, teams are widely used, and team players are in high demand.

NATURE OF TEAMS

High-performing teams usually exhibit an overall team purpose, mutual accountability, collective work products, shared leadership roles, high cohesiveness, collaboration in deciding task assignments and procedures, and collective assessment of their own success. A team's performance can often be improved by the development of leadership skills and tools for running more effective team meetings. These include preparing an agenda, clarifying the objective, soliciting minority viewpoints, legitimizing questions and critical thought, testing the support for a tentative decision, and identifying specific action plans. In addition to these somewhat mechanical guidelines, *teamwork can be improved* by understanding a team's developmental stages, noting the ingredients for their success, and exploring the broad range of team leader behaviors that can facilitate their performance. Games play a valuable role in the process of building teamwork.

STAGES IN TEAM DEVELOPMENT

Especially in the creation of new teams, a number of critical questions need to be addressed. These include: "Who should be included?" "Whom can I trust?" "What guidelines will we follow?" "What contributions will each person make?" "Who will perform which roles?" and "How do we resolve conflicts?" As these questions emerge and are addressed, teams often evolve through a series of classic stages:

Forming: Team members share personal information, start to get to know and accept one another, and begin turning their attention toward the group's tasks.

Storming: Team members compete for status, jockey for positions of relative control, and argue about appropriate directions for the group. Tensions arise as individuals assert themselves.

Norming: The team begins moving together in a cooperative fashion, and a tentative balance emerges. Group norms evolve to guide individual behavior, and a cooperative spirit begins to blossom.

Performing: The team matures and learns how to handle complex challenges. Roles are performed and exchanged among members as needed, and tasks are efficiently accomplished.

Adjourning: Most committees, task forces, and short-term groups disband at some stage (but not necessarily ongoing teams). The breakup, called adjournment, requires dissolving intense social relations (letting go) and returning to permanent assignments.

The games in this book can be helpful at several different stages of the team development process. Some games help members get to know each other better. Some games encourage open sharing of thoughts and feelings. Other games provide team members with valuable problem-solving skill practice as they move toward becoming high-performing teams.

INGREDIENTS FOR TEAM SUCCESS

First and foremost, effective teams need a supportive environment. Team leaders encourage members to think like a team, give them adequate time for team meetings, and demonstrate faith in their ability to succeed. Team members must also have the necessary skills (and receive cross-training for other skills), obtain clarification of their expected roles, and identify some overall (superordinate) goal that will keep them passionately oriented toward achieving a mutual objective. Team rewards (items that are valued, perceived as possible to earn, and administered promptly when the group's goals are met) should also be provided. Most of all, team members need regular opportunities to interact with each other and learn from their interaction. Team building games are designed to provide those opportunities

TEAM BUILDING

Creating high-performance teams can be a challenging task, and it does not happen overnight. Typically, team leaders must rely on the process of *team building* to integrate individual skills and resources into a unified effort. Team building involves encouraging team members to examine closely how they currently work together, portraying ideal ways of collaborating, exploring the gaps and weaknesses they currently suffer from, and establishing action plans for implementing more effective ways of cooperating.

Team building does not usually happen by itself; it is best aided by someone who facilitates the process. A team leader, or *facilitator*, helps the group learn about itself, observes team meetings, feeds back key observations to the team, and sometimes confronts individuals by asking them to examine their behavior and its consequences (or explore new alternatives). The facilitator probes, questions, listens, watches for nonverbal cues, and stimulates problem solving. The intended results include a team that is open to new alternatives, aware of its own diverse resources, able to think and act independently, and willing to explore the consequences of their current or proposed actions.

THE BENEFITS OF TEAM BUILDING GAMES

Working in teams is hard work. It can be frustrating for members when discussions wander off the subject, when no agenda has been set or followed, or when meetings drag on interminably. Effort is wasted, energies sag, and boredom sets in. How can you inject team meetings with renewed enthusiasm, lift team spirit, and build the morale of team members?

We (and hundreds of thousands of users) have found that *games can be a magical antidote to boredom.* Games include a wide variety of activities, exercises, and icebreakers that make team meetings more fun, draw out feelings and emotions, and lift the spirits of team members. They have been used to supplement and upgrade team building sessions ever since it was discovered that people have very short attention spans. Participants respond much better when meetings have life, variety, and surprises! Today's workforce *expects* team meetings to be lively, fast-paced, innovative, participative, and imaginative. Games can materially help accomplish those objectives by focusing attention on the needs of the attendees.

Specifically, team building games can help accomplish these objectives:

Games help the team leader to *make a point*—one that is clear, memorable, and relevant to the task at hand. They are, in effect, powerful teaching tools for driving home a key idea.

Games help *build team morale.* They provide a sharp contrast to "business as usual" by injecting an element of competition, cooperation, and/or fun into team meetings.

Games help team members learn to *trust each other.* They provide opportunities for sharing insights, feelings, and experiences as the team develops common solutions. Increased understanding and appreciation for each other's inputs are valuable by-products.

Games help team members *become more flexible and adaptive.* Members soon understand and appreciate the fact that there may be more than one way to solve a problem.

Games provide opportunities for team leaders to *reinforce appropriate member behaviors.* When cooperation is displayed, when creativity is demonstrated, or when interpersonal barriers begin to break down, a leader can show appreciation for the desirable responses elicited from a team building game.

CHARACTERISTICS OF TEAM BUILDING GAMES

The unique features of games make them usable and appropriate for use in many team meetings and team building sessions. For example, games usually:

1. *Are quick to use.* They can range from a one-minute activity to an exercise that stimulates a one-hour discussion of its implications. However, since the activity should be used to add to or supplement the main purpose or content of the team meeting, the time devoted to the game should be tightly controlled. Most of the games in this book can be completed in 5-10 minutes, but they can be extended through alternative questions.

2. *Are inexpensive.* In general nothing has to be purchased, nor does an outside facilitator or consultant need to be hired. With few exceptions, the games included in this book can be used—again and again—at little or no cost by almost any team leader.

3. *Are participative.* To be used effectively, the games should involve the team members physically (through movement) or psychologically (through visual or mental activity or thought). Games typically help people focus their attention and make them think, react, speak, and (most importantly) have fun while learning how to be better team players.

4. *Use props.* Several of the games involve the use of a single prop or outside material to add realism and variety to the activity. These props could be as simple as a picture, a person, an inanimate object, or a handout.

5. *Are low-risk.* All the games in this book have been field-tested dozens of times in a variety of sessions with a variety of different groups and teams. When matched to the proper content, the right context, the right people, and the right climate, and when used in a positive manner, they will always work for you. The games are user-friendly, and people respond to them positively. There are almost no risks involved; they are proven effective and have no known adverse consequences.

6. *Are adaptable.* The best activities, like the best humorous stories, can be adapted to fit almost any situation, and still reinforce the points you want to make in your team building session. These games can be modified slightly to fit your tastes, and they'll retain their original flavor and character. In fact, it is highly recommended that you tailor the game as much as possible to fit your goals, your group, or your organization.

7. *Are single-focus.* The games in this book are designed to demonstrate or illustrate one major point or to accomplish one significant purpose. As such, they are oriented to micro issues rather macro issues. Keep them simple and focused, and they will do their job for you.

SUMMARY

Team building games are designed to help team leaders transform a group of loosely connected employees into a dynamic and productive team—a process that seldom occurs naturally. These games relieve boredom, lift team spirit, increase team morale, and re-energize team members. They provide a brief break from an intensive focus on team tasks, and serve as an important adjunct or supplement to a team meeting. They can help move a set of individuals forward in their team development process, and simultaneously provide important answers to a variety of critical questions that team members are facing. Games help make team meetings more fun, and we believe that is a *very* worthy objective.

We have consistently found that even inexperienced team leaders can use the games in this book with confidence after minimal preparation. Team members are likely to become highly engaged, and respond to each game with enthusiasm and appreciation. They will learn how to identify key learning points, reinforce each other's contributions, and be stimulated to search for ways to translate their new insights and skills to work-related interactions. Best of all, the games in this book are typically quick to use, inexpensive, participative, low-risk, adaptable, and highly focused. Try them, and you'll soon agree!

How to Use This Book

TEAM BUILDING GAMES ARE SIMPLE

Games comprise a special set of trust-building activities, illustrations, exercises for improving team spirit, or experiences designed and used to support the objectives of a team meeting. As discussed in "Introduction to Team Building Games," these games typically have many advantages: they are very brief, easy to use, inexpensive, highly engaging, field-tested, and virtually certain to produce a meaningful outcome. In fact, many of them provide a valuable lesson whether the participants "succeed" in a task or not, for the focus is often on the *process* they used, their discussion of it, and how that process can be applied to their team relations on the job.

For example, in your first team meeting, you may wish to try the classic "dollar exchange/idea exchange" exercise, which goes like this:

> *Ask for the loan of a dollar from a member of the team. Display it prominently in one hand, and proceed to ask for the loan of a second dollar from another person. Then carefully repay the first loaner with the second dollar and repay the second loaner with the first dollar. Now ask the rhetorical question, "Is either of these persons now richer than they were before?" (Neither, of course, is.) Then point out to the team that, by contrast, had two ideas been shared as readily, not only the respective givers, but all team members would be richer in experience.*
>
> *Now divide the team into two small groups. Assign one group these questions: What factors discourage us from sharing useful ideas and insights with other team members? How can we overcome or diminish these factors?*

Assign the other group these questions: What factors encourage us to share ideas with other team members? How can we increase these factors?

After a few minutes, ask a representative of each group to report on their discussions. Conclude the session by asking team members if they want to resolve to stop idea-discouraging behaviors and promote more idea-encouraging ways.

As you can see by this example, games (activities and exercises) for team building can be incredibly simple. This example illustrates just one of the possible uses of team building games—to convey the major message or theme of a particular moment. Used in this way, games increase the likelihood of members' retention of a lesson or skill while drawing on their intellect and creative abilities in a temporary departure from a more serious presentation of material. In short, games help team members have *fun* while learning a key *point*.

SELECTING AN APPROPRIATE TEAM BUILDING GAME

When you examine this book, you'll notice that each team building game has a distinctive purpose. These games can, however, be classified according to their general applications.

The following thirteen major questions parallel the major issues facing most developing teams. These questions are:

Who are "they"? In new teams, in particular, members need to establish a trust level with their counterparts. This requires finding out some key information—both personal and skill-related—about team members. Often, however, individuals need initial help in breaking through the protective facades of others, as well as disclosing relevant information about themselves. Games in this section are designed to help introduce members to each other and "break the ice."

Who are "we"? An ideal work group is far more than (and different from) a mere collection of talented individuals; it is a highly coordinated, mutual-trusting, high-performance *team.* This self-identification as a team does not come easily, or immediately. It requires effort and (often) time. Games in this area are designed to aid members in thinking of themselves as a team, creating a team identity, and building initial cohesiveness within the group.

Why should we be a team? New teams, especially those whose members have been "thrown" together, may carry self-doubt about not only their own capabilities but the capacity of a group of relative strangers to be highly effective. If one or more members lack the exhilarating experience of having been part of a high performing team, they may question the value of teamwork. This is especially true when they discover the substantial amount of effort that is required to build a team from scratch. The games in this section are oriented toward convincing members that two (or more) heads are indeed often better than one.

What if we aren't all alike? There is a wealth of "gold" in the background that each person brings to the team. However, this rich lode of diversity can be mined only if the members know where to look and if they are ready to appreciate what they may find. Diversity within teams is a powerful asset, but it needs to be managed for the benefit of all members and the team in total. Team building games can help members uncover the less obvious ways in which they differ from each other, and plant the seeds of exploration into how those differences may be productively used.

Whom do we trust? Teams without trust are overly cautious at best, and suspicious and sabotage-prone at their worst. Without trust, members retreat into their emotional "shells," much as a turtle withdraws its body into its protective shell when it senses imminent attack. The task of a team leader is to create a climate of openness and constructive confrontation that will build trust among group members. Games can provide a useful vehicle for stimulating this behavior in a "safe" task-based environment.

Where are we going, and what is our route? From a self-managing perspective, teams need to confront two central issues: Where are we going (team goals), and how are we best going to get there (team norms)? Although goals and objectives for a team are often implicit or taken for granted, there is a clear need to clarify the team's role and mission. Following this, team members need to hold an open and frank discussion about the types of behavior that are acceptable (desired) and unacceptable (dysfunctional). The games in this section are among the most powerful ones available for inducing members to converge on a single direction, as well as to initiate some action planning and norm development.

How are we doing? After a period of time, work teams sometimes become stagnant, plateau in their performance levels, and fail to progress further in their collaborative efforts. On those occasions, it is helpful for members to step back from the immediacy of task demands and ask themselves some key questions. For example, they might inquire, "Why are some teams cohesive and ours is not?" "Why do other teams seem to be instantly productive, while ours moves only slowly in that direction?" The challenge here is to stimulate team members to look at themselves, and uncover the problems that they might be having. The games in this section are useful stimulants for legitimizing candid conversation about what it means to be a team, providing an opportunity for taking an inventory of a team's strengths and resources, and monitoring the relative success of team development efforts.

How can we do things differently? Team members sometimes fall into behavioral "ruts" and need to break out of their old operating habits and paradigms. The leader's challenge is to get them to look for problems and to adopt new ways of thinking, acting, and solving problems. These are challenging tasks, and they won't be solved in a single session. Nevertheless, it is important that team members accept the importance of being creative, recognize their own limitations, and search for new ways to solve existing problems. The team building games in this section provide opportunities for members to stretch their minds and approach problems from a different perspective.

Can we get along better? One of the major obstacles to the creation of high-performance teams lies in interpersonal irritations that serve to distance people from each other. At an extreme, open animosity among members may even emerge, and this can instantly (if not irreparably) fracture the team's cohesiveness. In its place, teams need to demonstrate at least a minimum degree of cooperation. You may believe that your team members aren't as collaborative and compatible as you would like them to be, and therefore find the games in this section especially appropriate for developing the values of sharing, caring, and community building.

How can we work together better? Sometimes teams work too hard for their own good, and run the risk of "burning out." At other times, team meetings become repetitious and members no longer seem to have the energy to interact constructively with each other. At these moments, it is helpful for a team leader to draw from a set of games that are designed to stimulate broader participation among team members, encourage honest feedback from member to member, break down inhibitions among members, or simply give the team a success experience together. The games in this section will prove helpful at energizing the team to devote more effort toward the task.

What lies ahead? These are turbulent, chaotic, "white-water" times requiring anticipation of problems and flexible responses to them. However, large organizations (sometimes characterized as "elephants" or "giants") often seem resistant to change, and this resistance can permeate small teams as well. How can you get group members to accept the need for change, develop the skills to do so, and begin to act on that need? Some games are designed to contribute to the development of adaptive, change-oriented teams that are more likely to accept (and even seek) change in themselves and others.

How can we have more fun? There is some evidence that a work environment that embraces humor and occasional laughter produces higher performance. If team members focus exclusively on task achievement, tempers may eventually flare from the stress and destructive emotions may erupt. Occasionally it is wise, then, to set aside the team's task for a few moments and engage the members in a more light-hearted moment. One way to do this is to introduce brief "brainteasers" into a team meeting. These highly engaging word games still let people stretch their minds, but allow them to do so on playful tasks while they compete with the puzzle's creator.

How can we reinforce each other? The value of positive reinforcement for sustaining productive results is firmly established. Unfortunately, team members sometimes forget to share praise and reinforcement with each other. The games in this section will encourage members to remember how essential a positive self-image is (in themselves and others), practice giving positive strokes to their colleagues, and solicit (and gracefully accept) positive feedback from valued others.

Key Questions in Building

1. Who are they?
2. Who are we?
3. Why should we be a team?
4. What if we aren't all alike?
5. Whom do we trust?
6. Where are we going, and what is our route?
7. How are we doing?
8. How can we do things differently?
9. Can we get along better?
10. How can we work together better?
11. What lies ahead?
12. How can we have more fun?
13. How can we reinforce each other?

PREPARING GAME MATERIALS

You will find it helpful to maintain a supply of basic tools that are often used in team building games. Index cards, wide-tipped felt pens, newsprint pads, masking tape, play money, a "Nerf" ball, a deck of playing cards, paper clips, envelopes, a box of matches, a ball of string, or a few old neckties may all prove useful at some stage. In particular, it is valuable to look ahead and anticipate which games may be appropriate for a given meeting. After selecting one or more games, much time can often be saved by preparing the appropriate handout, transparency, or flip chart in advance.

INTRODUCING A GAME

In general, a brief explanation and background for a game should be given. It is important to *provide a context for the activity*—a framework to aid the team members see where it fits into the day's agenda. Get their undivided attention, solicit their cooperation, and share appropriate information with them. Then assign them their task, and clearly specify the time limits to be adhered to. It is imperative that the interaction be monitored, and group discussion be ended on schedule.

LEADING A TEAM DISCUSSION

Games will remain just that—games—in the absence of effective facilitated discussion. Look over the entire set of materials provided. Anticipate probable results and reactions. Prepare not only the questions provided, but also additional ones that allow you to tailor the results to your own organization. Indicate the time limits available for discussing the game. Focus intensively on the meaning and purpose of a game (one of the thirteen objectives), while minimizing conversation on the mechanics of the game itself. Make the participants responsible for generating meaningful conclusions; don't be too quick to insert your own opinions and observations. Keep the discussion flowing rapidly, and terminate it when all major points have been brought to light.

MAKING THE TRANSITION TO APPLICATIONS

All of the games provided here are generic, meaning that they are broad in nature and not restricted to any one organization or industry. It is imperative that you shift the team's attention from a focus on *what* happened in the game to clear attention on what it *means* and what its *significance* is. Encourage participants to consider questions like "What will I (we) remember from the game tomorrow? What does it illustrate about our own team's behavior? How can we use it to improve our team performance?" Then make a record of the key learning points raised and the action plans developed, and distribute it to the team for later review and action.

TIPS FOR USING TEAM BUILDING GAMES

After more than two decades of experience with designing and conducting team building games, we have learned a number of important lessons. Although the guidelines we present here appear to be incredibly simple, they are vitally important to your success. We urge you to study these four generic rules carefully and follow them closely.

1. *Select the specific game carefully.* This requires scanning the entire set of games for each objective identified earlier so as to develop reasonable familiarity with the nature and requirements of each before choosing one or more for use with your team. Final selection should include consideration of whether the particular game fits your team's general nature and character, the objectives for the team's meeting, and the participants themselves.

2. *Have an objective.* Some persons jump into using a game but lack a well-thought-out, clearly articulated idea of what they hope to accomplish with it. Simply put, they lack an objective— the logical starting point. As a result, many of them use a game only (and inappropriately) because it was available, handy, or looked interesting. You *must* do a high-quality job of selecting games that fit your objectives—and then communicate that purpose to the team members.

3. *Have a back-up plan.* If you believe in Murphy's law ("What can go wrong probably will!"), it would be wise to have more than one game available. Similar to having a "Plan B" to use if

"Plan A" doesn't work, a team leader should learn the wisdom of developing a back-up plan. Remember that a prop may break, the team may have "played" that particular game just last week while you were on vacation, or the team may prove to be unresponsive to a certain type of game. Be ready with an alternative.

4. *Pretest the game.* A skeptic once advised people to trust no one's promises except those from God and "even then make sure that you get it in writing!" Heeding this ultraconservative advice, game users should not rely totally on the description provided with the game, or someone else's recommendation of it as a surefire winner. Ideally, you should find some safe context for experimenting with it before possibly wasting the team's time and energies on it. Close colleagues, volunteer staff, or family members are remarkably good critics. Use them.

In addition to the four general guidelines just provided, we offer you ten additional rules for the use of games in team building.

1. *Choose low-risk activities.* You should always take care not to offend your team members. Do not place them at unnecessary levels of physical or psychological risk. Never purposely antagonize the team members. Always screen the games so that you can feel comfortable knowing it is a "can't miss" experience.

2. *Be brief and selective.* Time is a vital resource, and organizations can't afford to waste it. The majority of the games presented here can be introduced and used in relatively short time periods. However, tips are also provided indicating how to expand upon the discussion if that proves desirable. Always remember that the game is *not* the major part of the team building session. It is only an aid to achieve your other results and goals. Don't drag the game out, and don't use too many within a single session. Think of games as an appetizer or dessert, but not as the main course of a meal. Games are a means to a serious end, but not an end in themselves.

3. *Be creative.* Experiment a little. Search for ways to *adapt* or tailor a game to best fit your purpose for the team at hand. Always be on the lookout for new ways to make your point within a meeting. Stay flexible.

4. *Evaluate your use of games.* Keep close tabs on the frequency with which you use games with a team, the game's apparent impact on the team's learning and retention, and the team's reaction to/reception of your games. It is all too easy to fall into ruts, such as using the same games again and again in subsequent meetings, or even overusing games and exercises to the detriment of the intended message. Audit yourself on your use of games, and resolve to update and expand your repertoire of games.

5. *Lighten up.* Keep in mind all the caveats and guidelines explained above. Take your task seriously, but don't take yourself too seriously. Team members will be even more on your side when they detect that you are a "real" person—someone who can laugh at yourself and allow minor deviations from a structured exercise. Above all, have fun, and make it fun for the team!

Guidelines for Team Building Games

General Rules:
1. Select them carefully.
2. Have an objective.
3. Have a back-up plan.
4. Pretest the game.

Tips for Team Building:
1. Choose low-risk activities.
2. Be brief and selective.
3. Be creative.
4. Evaluate your use of games.
5. Lighten up.
6. Don't use games just to entertain.
7. Be prepared.
8. Know the answer.
9. Anticipate some resistance.
10. Anticipate recall of the game, not the message.

---

6. *Don't use games just to entertain.* High-performance teams want to be productive and use their time wisely; don't waste valuable meeting time by using a game solely to entertain.

7. *Be prepared.* After deciding to use a game, prepare for it thoroughly; never select one at the last minute. Make certain that you are totally familiar with it, your goals are clearly defined, and you have a definite plan for debriefing the team at the game's conclusion so as to clearly illustrate the points brought forth.

8. *Know the answer* (if one exists). There is tremendous value in preparing a visual "key" that could be pulled out and displayed if our minds should go blank while under pressure. Prepare a written "job aid" and keep it handy.

9. *Anticipate some resistance.* You may occasionally encounter some team members who believe that games are "silly." If so, we suggest that you provide a clear explanation of the purpose of the activity, enlist the team's help in making it work, and promise them that the meaning will become clear during the debriefing.

10. *Anticipate recall of the game, not the message.* Because games are "different" from a classic work-oriented agenda, there is always a temptation for members to remember the game or activity and forget the underlying message. Once the game is completed and the meeting is nearly over, turn the group's attention once more to the key learning points, where the emphasis needs to be placed.

DANGER ZONES IN USING GAMES

We *want* you to succeed in your use of games for team building. Therefore, we need to provide a balanced perspective on games by identifying some of the disadvantages and pitfalls to offset the enthusiasm that we have been exhibiting throughout these introductory sections. The following comments identify a series of potential difficulties or limitations, many of which can be minimized through careful planning and adequate preparation.

**Danger Zones in
the Use of Games**

1. Props needed
2. Time requirements
3. Preparation
4. Simplistic image
5. Inappropriate usage
6. Distraction from learning
7. Overly complicated
8. Personally threatening

---

1. *Props.* Some games require the use of props. Although these are usually simple and conveniently available, a few may prove to be inconvenient to obtain on short notice or assemble in a hurry, especially without adequate lead time before the session in which they will be used.

2. *Time.* A few games, or extended versions of existing games, can involve more extended time requirements than you are willing to devote. It is incumbent upon you to chart the process, tightly structure the discussion, and know when to call a halt.

3. *Preparation.* Games vary in the depth of background required to conduct them properly. Some require no special preparation, while others may be enriched by one's unique educational background, in-depth reading, or expertise in group processing skills (i.e., drawing out the major points illustrated in the game via a spirited group discussion).

4. *Image.* Some games may be perceived as overly simplistic and sophomoric in nature by some participants, while being relevant and vivid to others. You need to gauge the sophistication of your group in relation to the game to be used, and perhaps pretest the proposed game on one or two participants.

In addition to these *structural* limitations, there are also some pitfalls in your use of games. It is possible that insecure, inexperienced, or unprepared individuals may use a game to kill time, to impress colleagues with how smart they are, or even to "put down" some team members by setting them up to fail on a game. Any time that playing games begins to dominate the focus of a team's interactive process, they should be used with less regularity. They are designed to be *supportive tools,* not the *purpose* of team meetings. Similarly, if most participants perceive that the games are "hokey" or cute, but are simultaneously distracting from the overall goal of the team meeting, more careful explanation and judicious use is in order. You should always encourage team members to demand (and contribute) answers to the ques-

---

Key Points to Remember

1. Sharpen your professional team leader skills by seeking and obtaining a balance between your emphasis on technical content (being *issue*-focused) and team process (*how* things are taking place). Seek to achieve balance between the two objectives.

2. Games are invaluable aids that can contribute not only to higher participant satisfaction with team meetings, but also to the creation of learning individuals and a learning organization (the team). This is a higher goal well worth striving for.

3. Games can help to "warm up" a team before it gets underway on its regular work agenda. Games can legitimize the involvement of all participants, introduce and illustrate a point more vividly, or close a team building session with high impact.

4. A broad array of games should be reviewed before selecting the most feasible one(s). Then they should be pretested and matched against the specific objectives for that specific team meeting. Outcomes should be anticipated, alternatives prepared, limitations recognized, and some plan for assessment of their success implemented.

---

tions of "So what?" or "What's in it for us?" for each game, and there should always be one (or preferably more) substantive answer. Finally, good games should not become overly complicated, nor should they in any way be allowed to become personally threatening or demeaning to any team member.

SUMMARY

Games can contribute to both the content and process objectives of a team meeting. Most importantly, they facilitate member learning and development of trust while also making the meeting itself more enjoyable. Games can be used:

As icebreakers.

To help create team identity.

To demonstrate the value of teamwork.

To stimulate the appreciation of diversity.

To build mutual support and trust.

To improve team functioning.

To stimulate the team members' recognition of the need for change.

To surface hidden problems.

To interject greater energy into team meetings.

Numerous guidelines have been presented to increase the likelihood of your first-time success. These guidelines are directed toward the selection, use, and evaluation of games, and are drawn from the experience of hundreds of applications. Above all, you are urged to keep games in their proper perspective, recognizing that most are designed to help improve some facet of team performance—and to interject a bit of fun in the process. Enjoy!

The BIG Book of
Team Building
Games

1

Icebreakers

Getting to Know Each Other Better

GETTING TO KNOW YOU

OBJECTIVES

To get to know teammates.

To build trust among people who work together.

To develop a "personal profile sheet" on team members, colleagues, clients, or friends.

MATERIALS REQUIRED

Copies of "Getting to Know You" forms for each participant.

PROCEDURE

At a team meeting, explain that each team member has special skills, knowledge, and talents that will help to make the team stronger as a unit. When team members are aware of each other's strengths, the team can function more effectively.

Distribute one copy of the form that appears on page 5 to each team member.

Collect the completed forms, duplicate them, and bring copies for each team member to the next meeting.

The record keeping and updating can be done either manually (e.g., hard copy in a three-ring binder) or stored on a personal computer.

IF YOU HAVE MORE TIME

At a team meeting, distribute one copy of the form to each member. Ask members to pair up and conduct 5-minute interviews of each other, using the "Getting to Know You" form as a worksheet. Tell members to be prepared to introduce their partners to the rest of the group by spotlighting 3 interesting pieces of information learned during the interview.

If you wish to store the information in a three-ring binder or a computer database, do the following:

After the paired introductions, distribute blank copies of the forms and ask members to complete the forms themselves. (This will ensure accuracy of the information.) Let team members know that you will collect their completed forms, duplicate them, and distribute them to other team members at the next meeting. Information that individuals don't want made known to the team or entered into a database should be omitted from the worksheet.

TIPS

Make any additional insertions or modifications to the form as you deem necessary.

When conducting the paired interviews, if the group is not divisible by two, ask one group to work as a trio. Tell the trio to allot 3 minutes per person for their interviews.

To keep the interviews on schedule, announce when the allotted time for each round of interviews has elapsed.

For the sake of accuracy, each individual should either personally complete the informational form that is to be distributed to the team or review the form prior to publication.

GETTING TO KNOW YOU

Name of Person Interviewed: _____

Job Title: _____

Spouse's Name: _____

Spouse's Employment or Activities: _____

Children's Names and Ages: _____

Hometown: _____

Person's Hobbies: _____

Spouse's Hobbies: _____

Favorite (or Dream) Vacation: _____

Best Accomplishments:

   Family: _____

   Personal: _____

   Childhood: _____

   Work: _____

Most Memorable Moments:

   Family: _____

   Personal: _____

   Childhood: _____

   Work: _____

Favorite Colors: _____

Favorite Holiday: _____

Favorite Food(s): _____

Strongest Feelings Shared during the Interview: _____

_____

_____

CANDID CAMERA:
LEARNING TO PUT FACES WITH NAMES

OBJECTIVES

To help the team leader(s) learn the names of team members.

To help team members learn each other's names.

MATERIALS REQUIRED

Instant-developing camera and film.

PROCEDURE

This may be most valuable, and most viable, for extended meetings (e.g., multi-day, weeklong, or programs that meet in periodic sessions across several weeks).

As new team members arrive, ask them to pose briefly for a head-and-shoulders photograph. Staple the instantly-developed picture to a biographical sheet for that person, which is then inserted into your own three-ring binder. (See, for example, the bio sheet in A Clear Image on page 21.) This is particularly useful for larger (over 15) teams or for team leaders who experience difficulty learning names! This allows you to review the bios and photos periodically prior to each session.

IF YOU HAVE MORE TIME

Type up (in large print) a roster of all team members in advance of the first meeting. Cut the names out, and tape them to a poster board, leaving space for the pictures. As individuals arrive, take their pictures and place them in the proper place on the poster. This not only helps you, but provides a "rogue's gallery" that members can refer to for identifying each other.

TIP

The bio sheets with pictures can be an invaluable tool for helping team members connect with each other by name at future sessions.

(SORT OF) GLAD TO MEET YOU

OBJECTIVE

To break the ice and to show how body language can contradict or reinforce verbal messages.

MATERIALS REQUIRED

None.

PROCEDURE

Ask the group to form subgroups of 5 people. They will be asked to "meet and greet" each other in four ways. They should sequentially assume that:

✔ They really don't want to meet the other person.

✔ They fear that the other might reject their greeting.

✔ They already know they are friends.

✔ They already know the other person—but just a little bit.

After each of the above four role plays is announced, allow 3–4 minutes for each activity so everyone can experience the activity. Then direct them to rotate to a new person and conduct the next role play.

DISCUSSION QUESTIONS

1. How did you feel the first time when you weren't really overly thrilled (to put it mildly) to be meeting the other person?
2. What influences you most when making first contact?
3. Did your nonverbal behavior reinforce or negate your words or feelings?

9

4. Why were the first two activities uncomfortable?

5. Can your nonverbal cues speak more loudly than your words? Are you conscious of your range of nonverbal signals?

TIP

Bring a Polaroid-type camera and take several candid photos of facial expressions and bodily gestures. Post these or pass them around for laughs to loosen up the team.

WILL THE REAL MR./MS. JONES STAND UP?

OBJECTIVE

To break the ice by forcing people to introduce themselves by means of their drawing ability, rather than their words.

MATERIALS REQUIRED

3 × 5 cards.

PROCEDURE

Individuals are asked to take out their business cards (if some don't have cards, provide them with 3 × 5 index cards).

On the back of the cards, ask them to draw a picture that describes themselves in any creative way. These can be sketches of themselves, their hobbies, jobs, interests, or family. Anything that can describe them is fair game!

Collect all the cards in a container.

A volunteer is chosen at random to pick out a card and look at the drawing, not the name side of the card.

The introducer then tells the group as much as possible about the card owner by interpreting the sketch, making any assumptions or inferences desired.

After each "introduction," the person who drew that sketch stands and clarifies, corrects, or more truthfully completes his or her introduction. That person then pulls out another card and proceeds to "introduce" that individual.

Continue the process until all persons are introduced.

DISCUSSION QUESTIONS

1. Why do we stick so closely to "just the facts" in our self-introductions—name, job, and employer?

2. How comfortable did you feel disclosing, through art, other aspects about yourself?

3. What were some of the more interesting things discovered?

If you suspect that team members will be reticent about interpreting others' drawings, you can volunteer to be first and provide a richly developed, previously prepared interpretation of a cohort's drawing (but it's best to warn the other individual first!).

People who don't consider themselves artistic may have reservations about creating a drawing and sharing it with others; so, preface the activity with the caveat that you don't have to be an artist to do this. Any rough sketch will do.

The time required depends on the number of participants.

✔ Allow 2–3 minutes for team members to draw their sketches.

✔ Allow 1 minute for each introduction and 1 minute for the person who was introduced to supplement the information.

✔ Allow 5 minutes for the team to discuss their observations and learning at the conclusion of the exercise.

SELF-DISCLOSURE INTRODUCTIONS—1

OBJECTIVES

To provide innovative ways of introducing members to each other.

To build team spirit by helping members to learn more about each other.

To help establish self-disclosure as a team norm.

MATERIALS REQUIRED

None.

PROCEDURE

Instruct participants to take two items (e.g., family pictures, credit cards, rabbits' feet) from their purses, wallets, or pockets.

When introducing themselves to the group, they should use whatever they took out to help describe themselves in at least two ways (e.g., "I am superstitious"; "I'm such a tightwad that this is the first dollar I ever earned").

TIPS

Allow 1 minute per person.

This activity is not limited to use with newly formed teams. It can also be effective as a meeting warm-up with established teams. When introducing the activity to groups whose members already know each other, point out that there is always something new team members can learn about each other that will increase rapport and make the team members aware of each other's strengths and applicable experiences.

IF YOU HAVE MORE TIME

Combine this activity with another one of the self-disclosure introductions.

SELF-DISCLOSURE INTRODUCTIONS—2

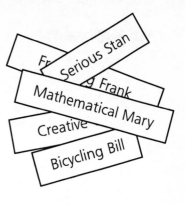

OBJECTIVES

To provide innovative ways of introducing members to each other.

To build team spirit by helping members to learn more about each other.

To help establish self-disclosure as a team norm.

MATERIALS REQUIRED

None.

PROCEDURE

Ask each team member to state his or her name and attach an adjective that not only describes a dominant characteristic, but also starts with the first letter of her or his name (e.g., Serious Stan, Mathematical Mary, Bicycling Bill, Creative Cathy, etc.).

TIPS

Allow one minute per person.

This activity is not limited to use with newly formed teams. It also can be effective as a meeting warm-up with established teams. When introducing the activity to groups whose members already know each other, point out that there is always something new team members can learn about each other that will increase rapport and make the team members aware of each other's strengths and applicable experiences.

Invite team members to explain how their chosen characteristic illustrates or improves the way they work.

Combine this activity with another one of the self-disclosure introductions.

SELF-DISCLOSURE INTRODUCTIONS–3

OBJECTIVES

To provide innovative ways of introducing members to each other.

To build team spirit by helping members to learn more about each other.

To help establish self-disclosure as a team norm.

MATERIALS REQUIRED

None.

PROCEDURE

Group members introduce themselves by name but also provide a nickname that they now have, once had, or would be willing to have if they could pick their own.

During breaks, members are encouraged to circulate and explore the reasons behind the announced nicknames.

TIPS

Allow 1 minute per person.

This activity is not limited to use with newly formed teams. It also can be effective as a meeting warm-up with established teams. When introducing the activity to groups whose members already know each other, point out that there is always something new team members can learn about each other that will increase rapport and make the team members aware of each other's strengths and applicable experiences.

IF YOU HAVE MORE TIME

Combine this activity with another one of the self-disclosure introductions.

A CLEAR IMAGE

OBJECTIVE

To acquaint new team members with one another in an informal setting.

MATERIALS REQUIRED

Chart or transparency with the question you intend to ask the group written on it.

PROCEDURE

Review the sample questions on the preprinted form provided.

Select one question. Write the question on the board or on a sheet of flip chart paper, or create an overhead transparency.

Ask each team member to write an answer to the question. Tell them the next step in the process is to introduce themselves to their teammates by sharing their answers to the question.

When the introductions have been completed, point out that these introductions have revealed "gut-level" values held by the team members.

DISCUSSION QUESTIONS

1. What did your answer to the question posed tell you about your values?
2. What commonalities in our values were revealed by our answers?
3. What differences in our values were revealed by our answers?
4. How can we divide team responsibilities so that assignments are compatible with each individual's values, as well as his or her expertise, skills, and abilities?

IF YOU HAVE MORE TIME

Give each team member a preprinted form as shown on the following page. After allowing a few minutes to respond to the questions, ask team members to introduce themselves. These introductions will reveal "gut-level" values held by the individuals.

A CLEAR IMAGE

On any team, one of the most difficult, yet important, steps is to become acquainted with the other members. To make the job of introducing yourself a little easier, take a few minutes and consider the following statements. We've left space for you to scribble down some thoughts and ideas. It's fair to peek at this later when you are addressing the other people.

1. Who am I? _____

2. What I value most is: _____

3. What motivates me is: _____

4. What I like most about my job is: _____

5. What I like least about my job is: _____

6. Money, time, and responsibility aside, I would rather be doing _____

_____ more than anything else.

7. Excluding my parents, if I could choose any two people for parents, they

would be: _____

2

Who Are We?

Creating Team Identity

SO MUCH IN COMMON

OBJECTIVES

To demonstrate that people often have more in common than **not** in common.

To create team identity.

MATERIALS REQUIRED

Copies of the Commonality Exercise form.

PROCEDURE

Distribute copies of the Commonality Exercise Form to each team member. Ask team members to find a partner quickly. When given the signal to begin, instruct them to find out as many things as they possibly can that the two of them have in common. Ask them to write down the partner's name and jot down, in the first column, the items that they found to be in common.

At the end of 2–3 minutes, call time and ask team members to find a new partner and, at your signal, repeat the process. Call time after 2–3 minutes.

DISCUSSION QUESTIONS

1. How many of you found more than 15 things in common?
2. What were some of the unusual items you discovered?
3. How did you uncover these areas of commonality?
4. Is it likely that in most situations, we may well find similar results, i.e., we have much more in common than we otherwise might think?
5. What implications does this have for us as members of a team? Of a diverse workforce?

TIPS

The noise level can get high during this exercise. Blow a whistle or ring a bell to signal the end of each round.

To speed up the exercise, shorten the Commonality Exercise form from 15 items to 7 or 10 items.

To make the activity fun, give prizes to the 2 people who found the most in common. Have extra prizes in case of a tie.

IF YOU HAVE MORE TIME

Repeat the process one more time.

COMMONALITY EXERCISE

List the things you find in common with three other people in the workshop.

NAME _____	NAME _____	NAME _____
1 _____	1 _____	1 _____
2 _____	2 _____	2 _____
3 _____	3 _____	3 _____
4 _____	4 _____	4 _____
5 _____	5 _____	5 _____
6 _____	6 _____	6 _____
7 _____	7 _____	7 _____
8 _____	8 _____	8 _____
9 _____	9 _____	9 _____
10 _____	10 _____	10 _____
11 _____	11 _____	11 _____
12 _____	12 _____	12 _____
13 _____	13 _____	13 _____
14 _____	14 _____	14 _____
15 _____	15 _____	15 _____

TEAM DISCOVERY

OBJECTIVES

To create team identity by helping members to discover more about each other.

To establish asking for information and self-disclosure as team norms.

MATERIALS REQUIRED

None.

PROCEDURE

Ask the team members to brainstorm a list of provocative questions they would like to have each other answer (and that they would be willing to answer). Write these down in front of the group.

Have them screen the list to delete those in questionable taste, and select the 2–3 that everyone feels most comfortable with.

Proceed to have each team member provide answers to the questions.

TIP

Allow 1 minute for each person to give his or her answers.

PORTABLE SKILLS

OBJECTIVES

To create team identity and build team spirit by helping members to learn more about each other.

To establish self-disclosure as a team norm.

MATERIALS REQUIRED

3 × 5 cards, pins or tape.

PROCEDURE

Explain that skills are portable and every member of the team is bringing a briefcase or box full of knowledge and skills to the team. This next activity will help us to discover individual strengths that will make us a productive team.

Distribute 3 × 5 cards.

Ask participants to write their names on the cards and below their names list two specialties or skills that they bring to the team, e.g., knowledge of statistical process control, organizational skills, or proposal writing.

When participants complete the cards, have them pin, tape, or hold the cards up in front of them as they circulate in the room, allowing others to engage them in exploratory conversations about the items.

This activity illustrates that there is always something new team members can learn about each other that will increase rapport and make the team members aware of each other's strengths and applicable experiences.

THE JOY OF SIX

OBJECTIVE

To provide a vivid demonstration of the satisfaction (joy) of being included in a group (of six), and the uneasiness of being excluded.

MATERIALS REQUIRED

Sufficient messages and envelopes, prepared in advance, to accommodate all participants.

PROCEDURE

Prepare a series of short sayings (e.g., "The customer is number one") and make 6 copies of each. Ideally, the messages should relate either to the central topics of the meeting or else to currently important themes or issues in the organization, such as "Coping with Change."

Make single copies of 1–5 other messages. Place each of the sayings in an individual (unmarked) envelope, seal the envelopes, and mix them up. Give one envelope to each member.

Instruct members to open their envelopes, read the messages, circulate around the room, introduce themselves, and repeat the message (softly). When an individual finds someone else with the same message, they are to team up. Tell them to continue this search and introductory process, staying in growing clusters, until they are all in teams of 6 persons (i.e., experiencing the "joy of six").

When all but the "loners" are in their groups of six, act surprised and then lead the team in the following discussion.

DISCUSSION QUESTIONS

1. How does it feel to not be accepted into a group or team? Does this ever happen in your jobs? Is it intentional?

2. How did it feel when you found someone with the same message?

3. Why didn't those persons already in a team reach out to the excluded persons? How do organizational policies, or our own self-interests, prevent us from including others?

4. What can we do to include others "in the loop"?

5. What lessons does this have for team building?

TIP

If time is critical, or the group is large, reduce the number for each team to three or four.

WHAT'S OUR NAME? LOGO? SLOGAN?

OBJECTIVES

To create team identity.

To allow team members the opportunity to develop productive working relationships.

MATERIAL REQUIRED

Flip chart paper and markers for each group.

PROCEDURE

Lead the team in brainstorming ideas for a team name. Limit the time allowed to 5 minutes.

Upon completion of the game, save the name (and logo and slogan, if developed) and attempt to use it consciously at work in the future.

DISCUSSION QUESTIONS

1. How did you select your team name? Logo? Slogan? What criteria did you using to complete each of those three tasks?

2. How do you now feel about your team? Will it be more successful in its future tasks? Will it be personally satisfying to work in it?

3. What is the value of spending some time creating team identity? What is the cost?

IF YOU HAVE MORE TIME

Ask the team to develop a graphic logo (trademark) that will usefully portray who and what they are to the rest of the world. Allow 10 minutes for this activity, and then ask the team to provide a brief explanation of what the logo represents (if it is not clear). The logo should be drawn on the flip chart paper.

Then ask the team to develop a slogan (12 words or less) that they could use in public advertising. This slogan should identify whatever assets or attributes the team realistically thinks are most important and present within themselves. Allow 10 minutes for this activity, and then ask the team to explain what they hope their slogan conveys about themselves.

TIP

Sometimes a team has difficulty getting started on a creative task. Have a least one example of a team name, team logo, and team slogan available to stimulate their creative thinking.

3

What Can Teamwork Achieve?

Demonstrating Its Value

ANYTHING I CAN DO, WE CAN DO BETTER

OBJECTIVE

To demonstrate the value of team decision making.

MATERIALS REQUIRED

One copy of the Important Job Factors handout for each participant.

PROCEDURE

Distribute a copy of the Important Job Factors form on page 41 to each participant. Instruct them to rank order the 10 items from 1–10 (1 = highest; 10 = lowest) according to the degree to which they think workers nationwide considered that reason "very important" in deciding to take their current jobs. Results should be entered in column 2.

Ask them to repeat the ranking process working as a team. Instruct them to agree upon a team ranking and place the team responses in column 4.

Display the key on a transparency, and have team members enter the actual rankings in column 3 of their sheets. Then have them do the following:

1. Compute the absolute arithmetic differences (without regard to positive or negative sign) between their individual rankings in column 2 and the survey rankings in column 3, and write the answers in column 1.

2. Compute the absolute arithmetic differences (without regard to positive or negative sign) between the team's rankings in column 4 and the survey rankings in column 3, and write the answers in column 5.

3. Add up the absolute numbers in columns 1 and 5 and write the two totals in the space provided at the bottom of columns 1 and 5.

In the discussion that follows, point out that when you have the benefit of diverse viewpoints within teams, you usually make better decisions than when acting alone.

DISCUSSION QUESTIONS

1. Who performed better, individuals or the team?
2. How many of you were surprised by the differences between your individual rankings and the actual survey results?
3. What factors may have contributed to the differences between your individual rankings and the survey results?
4. How much more or less accurate were your rankings when you performed the ranking as a team rather than as individuals?
5. What factors contribute to team success on tasks such as these?
6. How can our team be used more productively?

IMPORTANT JOB FACTORS

DIRECTIONS:

Step 1. Individual Exercise. In column 2, rank order the following items from 1 to 10 (1 = highest; 10 = lowest) according to your estimate of the degree to which workers nationwide believed that reason to be "very important" in deciding to take their current jobs.

Step 2. Team Exercise. In your team, repeat the ranking process and arrive at a group ranking. Place the group ranking numbers in column 4.

Step 3. In column 3, enter the actual survey ranking results when the leader gives them to you.

Step 4. Compute the absolute arithmetic differences between each of your individual item rankings (column 2) and the key (column 3), without regard to positive or negative sign. Write the answers in column 1.

Step 5. Compute the absolute arithmetic differences between each of the team's item rankings (column 4) and the key (column 3), without regard to positive or negative sign. Write the answers in column 5.

*Step 6. Add up the totals of columns 1 and 5 and enter the totals in the spaces at the bottom of the grid. Note that **small** column totals indicate closer agreement with the nationwide study data.*

	Column				
	1	2	3	4	5
Advancement opportunity					
Control over work content					
Flexible work schedule					
Fringe benefits					
Job security					
Nature of the work					
Open communication					
Salary/wages					
Size of organization					
Stimulating work					
Totals:					

41

KEY: IMPORTANT JOB FACTORS

	Rank
Advancement opportunity	8
Control over work content	3
Flexible work schedule	7
Fringe benefits	6
Job security	4
Nature of the work	2
Open communication	1
Salary/wages	9
Size of organization	10
Stimulating work	5

Source: "Workforce Study Finds Loyalty Is Weak," *Wall Street Journal,* Sept. 3, 1993, p. B-1.

THE JIGSAW PUZZLE

OBJECTIVES

To stimulate participants to acquire and use a simple metaphor or paradigm for the characteristics of effective teams and organizations.

To demonstrate the value of group effort.

MATERIALS REQUIRED

Transparency of jigsaw puzzle pieces.

PROCEDURE

Show a transparency of the pieces of a jigsaw puzzle to the group. Ask them to list all the ways in which the jigsaw is similar to the composition and operation of a high-performance team.

Some of the many possibilities include:

1. There are boundaries (the straight-edged pieces).
2. Each piece plays a specific role in the solution.
3. Pieces are highly interconnected when teamwork occurs.
4. Each piece is unique in its nature (similar to the individual differences among people).
5. The solution is a fragile one (easily broken).
6. The whole is more (better) than the sum of its parts.
7. Some pieces are central, some are peripheral.
8. There are natural groupings (e.g., by color or design).
9. Pieces need someone to move them.
10. Rapid solution is aided by someone with an overall vision.

DISCUSSION QUESTIONS

1. Are you surprised by the number of similarities?

2. What are the ways in which you can use this metaphor?

3. What action guidelines does this point toward?

TIP

This exercise has a more powerful message if you distribute actual puzzle pieces (or a simple puzzle) to each team member, and let them experience the process of constructing it.

JIGSAW PIECES

JEOPARDY

OBJECTIVE

To reinforce information communicated during a team meeting.

MATERIALS REQUIRED

Previous preparation of test questions; prize.

PROCEDURE

Separate the team members into two groups.

Develop sets of test questions, organized in categories according to the items on the agenda.

Allow one group to select a category, and ask them a question. If they are successful, award a point (or play money may be used). If they are incorrect, the other group gets a chance to answer, and may thus earn points. If neither group gets the correct answer, they must look it up in their notes or the team leader can provide the correct answer.

The first group to accumulate a specified number of points is declared the winner (and some recognition or prize should be awarded).

The major benefits provided by this format are:

a. Repetition of key information presented at the meeting;

b. Reinforcement of effective learning;

c. Feedback to the team leader regarding the points learned well, and those on which there was difficulty on recall.

TIP

Prepare, in advance, a list of the major points you plan to cover in the team meeting prior to the Jeopardy exercise. Print these on a flip chart, cover each with a strip of paper, and reveal it as it is guessed in response to each question. This adds important visual reinforcement to the exercise.

THE TOP TEN TIME-WASTERS

OBJECTIVES

To demonstrate the value of group effort.

To provide a lighthearted opportunity for individuals or groups to test their knowledge of current business research regarding time-wasters.

MATERIALS REQUIRED

A transparency of the master list of time-wasters for managers; prizes.

PROCEDURE

This can be used either as a quick break during a concentrated meeting or as a device to draw team members' attention back to the meeting following a refreshment break.

Ask the members to identify the 10 most significant ways in which a manager's time is wasted. Individual quizzes can be distributed for this purpose.

Following the individual response period, group competition (i.e., breaking the team into two equal parts) works particularly well. In this way, no one feels embarrassed for not knowing some of the 10 items. Answers are generally discovered more rapidly, and the collective responses are usually more accurate than individual ones.

DISCUSSION QUESTIONS

1. How did you know the answers?
2. What helps us to retain information such as this?

3. Why might we block data such as this from our permanent brain storage?

4. How does this exercise demonstrate the merits of collective effort?

5. What ideas do you have for using time more effectively?

KEY: TIME-WASTERS FOR MANAGERS

1. Crises
2. Telephone calls
3. Poor planning
4. Attempting to do too much
5. Drop-in visitors
6. Poor delegation
7. Personal disorganization
8. Lack of self-discipline
9. Inability to say "no"
10. Procrastination

THE TOP TEN COMPANY-PAID HOLIDAYS

1.	Christmas Day
2.	Labor Day
3.	New Year's Day
4.	Independence Day
5.	Thanksgiving Day
6.	Memorial Day
7.	Day after Thanksgiving
8.	President's Day
9.	Day before or after Christmas
10.	Good Friday

OBJECTIVES

To demonstrate the value of group effort.

To provide a lighthearted opportunity for individuals or groups to test their knowledge of current business facts.

MATERIALS REQUIRED

A transparency of the master list of company-paid holidays; prizes.

PROCEDURE

This can be used either as a quick break during a concentrated meeting or as a device to draw participants' attention back to the meeting following a refreshment break.

Ask the members to identify the 10 most popular company-paid holidays. Individual quizzes can be distributed for this purpose.

Following the individual response period, group competition (i.e., breaking the team into two equal parts) works particularly well. In this way, no one feels embarrassed for not knowing some of the 10 items. Answers are generally discovered more rapidly, and the collective responses are usually more accurate than the individual ones.

DISCUSSION QUESTIONS

1. How did you know the answers?
2. What helps us to retain information such as this?
3. Why might we block data such as this from our permanent brain storage?
4. How does this exercise demonstrate the merits of collective (team) effort?

KEY: COMPANY-PAID HOLIDAYS

1. Christmas Day
2. Labor Day
3. New Year's Day
4. Independence Day
5. Thanksgiving Day
6. Memorial Day
7. Day after Thanksgiving
8. President's Day
9. Day before or after Christmas
10. Good Friday

(*Note:* Martin Luther King's birthday ranks as the next most frequent holiday.)

THE HAT PARADE

OBJECTIVES

To show that diverse interests and specialties make a team more balanced and effective.

To provide an unusual planning and organizing activity for a newly formed team or for a team that is about to take on a new project.

MATERIALS REQUIRED

Stick-on name tags for each person or a small card with sticking tape attached to it.

A list of project tasks or functions for each team member.

Optional: A collection of hats (the sillier the better), one for each team member. These can often be acquired inexpensively at secondhand shops or party stores (or make cardboard hats). Alternatively, ask each member to bring a distinctive hat to wear at the meeting.

PROCEDURE

Develop a list of tasks that must be accomplished or a list of functions that must be performed by various team members.

If you are using hats, give one hat to each person as they first enter the meeting room.

If members are wearing hats, ask them to model their hats for each other. (This often produces laughter as they feel silly and look around the room at others feeling silly.)

Distribute the list of tasks or functions. Ask team members to examine the list and select one task or function that particularly interests them, noting it on a small piece of paper or name tag and then sticking it on their jackets or on the front of their hats.

Explain that the task or function they have chosen will be their "specialist hat" for the day (or for the life of the project). While this is a team effort that requires cross-functional cooperation, each team member can take lead responsibility for his or her task or function.

Proceed with the meeting, reminding team members periodically of their chosen areas of expertise through questions like "Whose specialty hat is this topic?"

DISCUSSION QUESTIONS

1. What effect did designation as a lead person or subject-matter expert have on your attention to that topic during our meeting?

2. How can each of you apply your expertise in your chosen task or function to making our project a success?

3. How will our diverse interests and specialties make our team more balanced, stronger, or more effective?

4. Where are we weak and how can we supplement those areas?

5. What are potential areas of conflict that might arise from our diverse interests and perspectives?

6. What tasks or functions should be added to our list?

7. What tasks or functions should be deleted from our list?

8. What tasks or functions could be consolidated?

TIPS

Show an overhead transparency or a 2' x 3' chart displaying the list of tasks or functions. Be prepared to add to or delete from this list based on suggestions from team members during the meeting.

More than one member may have a strong interest in a particular task or function. In this case, ask one person to make a second choice.

If there are more people on the team than there are tasks or functions on the list, assign two or more individuals co-responsibility.

IF YOU HAVE MORE TIME

At the end of the meeting, split the team into twos, have them swap hats or name tags, and have each person brief or "train" the other (a "novice") in the specialty. Allow 5 minutes for each briefing, for a total of 10 minutes. If the group is not divisible by two, have one group work as a trio, and tell them they each have 3 minutes to brief the other two people on the specialty.

Reconvene the team and ask each person to share one thing learned as a result of the briefing received from partners. Allow 5 to 10 minutes for this debriefing.

KNOW YOUR CUSTOMER

OBJECTIVES

To illustrate the value of tapping the diverse knowledge and thinking styles of team members.

To serve as a meeting icebreaker or warm-up.

To accent the wealth that exists in customers if participants will just look for it.

MATERIALS REQUIRED

None, other than identifying an appropriate word for the group to analyze. You may wish to create a transparency of the key on page 65 that shows some of the possibilities for the word chosen.

PROCEDURE

Identify a key word that is relevant to your team meeting or central theme of the presentation. The example used here to illustrate the exercise is *Customer.*

Indicate to the group that their task, working alone, is to identify as many legitimate words as they can from the letters available to them, using each letter only once.

Ask them to make two predictions—the number of words they will individually identify, and the word score of the highest producer.

Then give them a tight time limit (e.g., 5 minutes) and start them on the task.

DISCUSSION QUESTIONS

1. How many words did you predict you'd find?

2. How does your own performance expectation compare to the expectations others held for themselves?

3. Did you exceed your own expectations or fall short? Why?

4. How many words did you predict could be found? How does this compare to the actual total?

5. How do you explain the actual results?

6. What does this exercise illustrate to you? (Are *customers* a rich source of information?)

TIPS

Members with high verbal skills typically do well on this activity. Those with lower verbal skills may experience some frustration. During the post-activity discussion, explain that some people are good with words, while others may be better with numbers or at analyzing spatial information. When all members contribute to the problem-solving process, both the team and the organization benefit.

If the topic of your meeting is sales or customer service, focus on the sales-oriented words within the word *customer* (e.g., use, user, more, store, cost). Point out that one of the elements of good customer service is knowing both the product and the customer.

KEY: WHAT'S IN (A) CUSTOMER?

Us	Ore	Or
Ort	Use	User
Rest	Rut	Rot
Rote	Rose	Cot
Cost	Cote	Come
Comer	Comes	Course
Cut	Cur	Core
Corset	Court	Sum
Some	Sore	Sot
Sour	Set	To
Tome	Tore	Tomes
To	Me	More
Mouse	Met	Must
Most	Toes	Tour
Custom	Costume	Costumer

JIGSAW TEAM-BUILDING

OBJECTIVE

To stress the importance of each team member's individual contributions, and the importance of working as a group.

MATERIALS REQUIRED

One previously constructed picture puzzle, divided into sets of approximately 10 pieces per participant, and then broken apart and allocated to each participant for reassembly.

Tape player with appropriate cassettes.

PROCEDURE

Select a solvable picture puzzle. Break it into subsets of 10 connectable pieces each. Distribute a subset to each participant (such that the subsets could then be connected to each other).

Instruct them to solve their own subset first, and then connect all the subsets appropriately until they have the total puzzle solved. Set a challenging time limit for task completion, and possibly play some energizing music (e.g., the *William Tell Overture*, or Wagner's *Ride of the Valkyries*) to create an additional sense of urgency.

You may choose to designate a small number of participants as free-floating troubleshooters who roam about the room and help those in trouble to see viable connections within their own subset and from one set to another.

DISCUSSION QUESTIONS

1. What reactions did you have when you realized your importance to the overall team?

2. What impact did the time deadline have on your effectiveness?

3. What was the impact of having team members available (and willing) to help you?

TIP

Watch the group dynamics for individualistic behaviors. For instance, some members may be reluctant to give up their puzzle pieces. Others may try to take control of all the pieces and attempt to do the assembly themselves. In your post-activity discussion, ask individuals to consider both their productive and counterproductive behaviors. It is likely that they are using the same behaviors in actual work situations, with similar positive or negative effects.

THE PARLOR GAME

OBJECTIVES

To demonstrate that teamwork gets better results than working alone.

To speed up any process involving familiarity with forms, tools, parts, materials, supplies, or equipment.

MATERIALS REQUIRED

Number and type of objects depends on program.

PROCEDURE

Assemble up to 15 portable objects related to work that the team is expected to accomplish; for example, computer parts, technical items, tools, manuals, forms, supplies, materials, office equipment, etc. Arrange them on a table hidden from view.

Group people into teams of 4 to 6. Explain that the objective is to work together to recognize the objects that will be used on the job.

Give each team 1 minute to view objects on the table in silence.

When groups have returned to their tables, have individuals write all they can remember in 2 minutes. Then have a team recorder make a master list to demonstrate that teamwork gets better results than working alone.

DISCUSSION QUESTIONS

1. How much more extensive were the team lists than the lists of each individual on the team?
2. What types of items were easiest for you to recall?

3. In this exercise, we saw how sharing knowledge with our teammates helped to make the team more productive. What other situations occur at work that would increase productivity if individual knowledge were shared with the team?

TIP

This game works well for employee orientation or for training individuals to work in cross-functional groups.

4

Who Can We Trust?

Building Mutual Support

I LIKE ME BECAUSE

OBJECTIVES

To build up the team members' self-esteem.

To build mutual support and trust.

MATERIALS REQUIRED

None.

PROCEDURE

Ask the group members to find a partner—preferably someone that they don't know well or would like to know better. Have them sit in chairs facing their partners.

Ask them to decide who will go first and then tell them to make eye contact with one another, get comfortable, maintain an open body position (don't cross arms, etc.), and speak to their partners about the topic "What do I like about myself?"

Let one person in each pair talk for 2 minutes. The passive partner cannot say a word, but through body language should express keen interest in the other person. At the end of 2 minutes, have them switch roles. Then the other partner—again without interruption—must talk for 2 minutes on "What I like about myself."

DISCUSSION QUESTIONS

1. What kinds of things do people like about themselves?
2. What kinds of things were noticeably *not* very frequently mentioned?
3. Why are we reluctant to express a positive self-image to others?

4. What are some relatively safe ways in which we can express our self-esteem at work?

5. What suggestions do you have for helping to build someone's self-esteem?

I'M OK, I REALLY AM!

OBJECTIVES

To build members' self-esteem and to stimulate empathetic listening.

To build mutual support and trust.

MATERIALS REQUIRED

Stick-on notepads for each small group.

PROCEDURE

Ask the group members to think about three eras of their lives—namely, their childhood years, when they were in school, and the current time. Tell them to think about each of these three time frames, and recall something that they did, or that happened to them, that really made them very proud. (Examples could be "when I was eighth-grade spelling champion," or "when I sold nine homes last month," etc.)

After each person has written down three things, form groups of 3 people. One person identifies the three proud moments in the three areas, and the person to the first speaker's right listens carefully to the comments and then must interpret briefly, for the other two, not what the first person *said*, but rather, what that person probably *meant*.

The third person (listener) makes no verbal comment, but takes a stick-on note and writes out a truthful and sincere compliment to the original speaker, verbally praises the speaker for those accomplishments, and attaches the stick-on note to the person's clothing. After the first round, the process is repeated with a second person reporting, another interpreting what the statements meant, and the third member writing out the compliment on a stick-on note. Repeat for the third person.

DISCUSSION QUESTIONS

1. How many feel comfortable praising yourselves?
2. How many periodically review past successes?
3. Do you know someone who can or will praise you?
4. How did it feel to have an empathetic listener?

TIP

Review with the team, either before or after the exercise, some simple ways to demonstrate empathetic listening.

A COAT OF ARMS

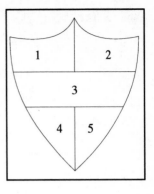

OBJECTIVES

To give group members the opportunity to describe qualities about themselves and to learn more about other members.

To build mutual support and trust.

MATERIALS REQUIRED

Copies of Coat of Arms on page 79, or blank sheets of paper.

PROCEDURE

Reproduce the coat of arms or ask members to draw a similar sketch.

Give the following instructions:

In space 1, draw something that characterizes a recent Peak Performance.

In space 2, sketch out something about yourself that very few people know.

Draw in space 3 a symbol of how you like to spend your spare time.

In space 4, fill in something you are very good at.

In space 5, write or draw something that epitomizes your personal motto.

After each person finishes, form pairs (preferably of members who don't know each other well), and have them try to identify what each other's coat of arms signifies.

Ask for several participants to describe their coats of arms to the group.

DISCUSSION QUESTIONS

1. What major themes were communicated?
2. Why do we tend to withhold information from others?
3. What does this exercise contribute to feelings of mutual trust?

COAT OF ARMS

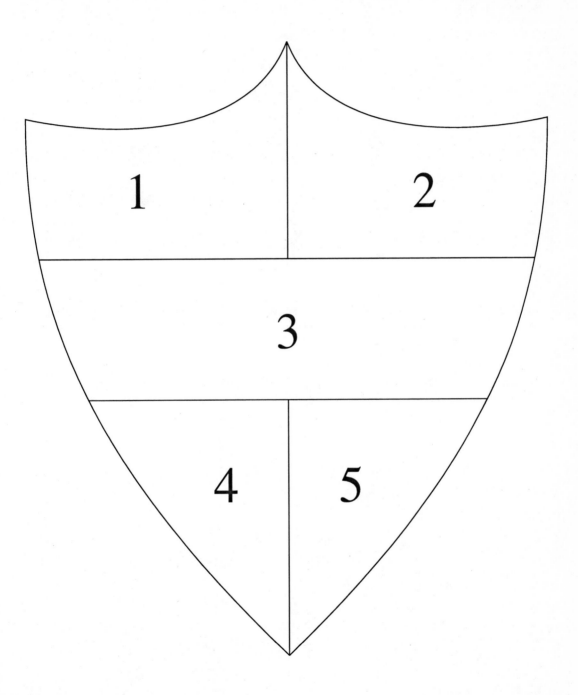

TRUST ME

OBJECTIVES

To demonstrate teamwork for support, leadership, and cooperation.

To build mutual support and trust.

MATERIALS REQUIRED

Bandanas.

PROCEDURE

Divide the group into teams of 4. Participation should be voluntary.

One person in each group is blindfolded; another is the leader who will verbally instruct the blindfolded person to go from Point A to Point B in the room or adjacent area. The leader must not touch the blindfolded person. The other two persons assist the leader and make certain the blindfolded person doesn't bump into anything.

When the walk (2–3 minutes) is completed, switch roles and repeat the exercise using a different route.

Repeat as time allows.

DISCUSSION QUESTIONS

1. How did you feel when blindfolded? (Uncertain, frightened, dumb, etc.)
2. Did you trust your leader? Why or why not?
3. Did you trust your coworkers? Why or why not?
4. What did you need when you were blindfolded? (Support, assurance, advice, etc.)

5. How does this activity apply to your organization? (Need help, counsel, affirmation, etc.)

6. How about your new team members? What lessons does this activity have for your relations with them?

TIPS

Be sure to make the area safe and clear of hidden obstacles.
Do *not* encourage haste or competition to see who can finish first.

5

How Should We Proceed?

Setting Team Goals and Norms

MOST? BEST? GREATEST?

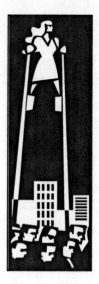

OBJECTIVES

To encourage disclosure of personal information among team members.

To develop a norm of sharing.

To break down facades.

To increase awareness of each other's experiences.

MATERIALS REQUIRED

None.

PROCEDURE

Select one provocative question for each meeting. You may choose either to announce it in advance (to give members time to think) or to introduce it on a spontaneous basis. To save time, ask each person to respond in 25 words or less.

Then call on each person to give his or her self-report. Examples of good questions include:

✔ What is your greatest achievement?

✔ What was the happiest day of your life?

✔ What is your most prized possession?

✔ What was the most fun you ever had?

✔ What is your dream vacation like?

✔ What is the best book you have ever read?

✔ Who is your most admired person?

✔ If you could have a T-shirt printed with a message, what would it say?

The whole purpose is to encourage lighthearted self-disclosure (on a superficial level) that lends itself to future follow-up and probing in casual conversation.

DISCUSSION QUESTIONS

1. Is it acceptable to disclose personal thoughts, dreams, values, or achievements during work?
2. What are the positive consequences of doing so?
3. What possible concerns do you have about doing so as a result of this exercise?
4. What norms are we creating by this exercise? Why didn't they exist before?

IF YOU HAVE MORE TIME

Make the team responsible for generating future questions by passing the assignment for picking the next question around within the group. You might even wish to record a "living history" of member responses by saving a key word or two from each person's response, and distributing a follow-up handout listing member names and themes.

TIPS

Keep it moving quickly.

You may wish to volunteer to be the first person to respond, to set the tone for the exercise.

To protect individuals from any embarrassment, you may wish to create a rule that members can pass on a question if they don't wish to answer.

TEAM BUILDING

OBJECTIVE

To allow team members to imagine their ideal project.

MATERIALS REQUIRED

Paper, flip chart.

PROCEDURE

Tell the team that they have just received a call from their operational vice president, human resource development officer, comptroller, information services officer, or similar authority that the organization has just allocated $_____ (an extremely high figure is suggested, e.g., $300,000) to be used strictly as the team identifies.

Give members 2 minutes to generate individual "wish lists," along with some approximate budget figure for each item. (An example could be to upgrade the team's computer system by purchasing new equipment and software. Costs would include new computers, monitors, printers, networking and group decision-making software, consulting fees, etc.)

Next, ask members to share the top priority item on their individual lists with the entire team. Post this information on a flip chart.

As a team, discuss the individual priority listings and attempt to arrive at consensus on a team list.

DISCUSSION QUESTIONS

1. If the team's top priority is really important, what are some ways we can convince the organization to budget the necessary dollars?

2. How forcefully did you make the case for your views?

3. How forcefully did others make the case for their views?

4. What are the team norms regarding expression of dissent, suppression of conflict, and methods of reaching consensus?

IF YOU HAVE MORE TIME

Divide the team into subsets of 4–5 persons each.

Ask each individual member of the small groups to work alone for 5–10 minutes and create a "wish list" with some approximate budget figure for each item.

Following 5–10 minutes of individual idea generation, each small group discusses the individual priority listings and attempts to arrive at consensus on a group list.

Each group prepares a flip chart and reports its results to the entire team.

With this longer version of the activity, you can ask the following discussion questions, in addition to questions 1–4 above.

✔ After you had written your individual "wish list," how many of you greatly altered your ideas or budgets as a result of your small group discussion?

✔ While group problem solving and decision making ordinarily produce a better result than individual efforts, are there some problems as well?

BESTS AND WORSTS

	Best	Worst
•	_____	• _____
•	_____	• _____
•	_____	• _____
•	_____	• _____
•	_____	• _____
•	_____	• _____
•	_____	• _____
•	_____	• _____
•	_____	• _____
•	_____	• _____
•	_____	• _____

OBJECTIVES

To help clarify group norms.

To set team goals.

To introduce complex topics in an enjoyable way.

MATERIALS REQUIRED

Newsprint, chalkboard, or screen and projector.

PROCEDURE

Ask team members to yell out the best and worst examples of the topic. For instance, identify the best and worst characteristics they know of teamwork, behavior in team meetings, or product or service quality.

Write the two lists on newsprint, chalkboard, or an overhead.

For each item on each list ask individuals to share reasons for placing that item on the list.

As a team, agree on the actions the team can take to be more effective based on the "best" list and one thing the team can stop doing from the "worst" list.

DISCUSSION QUESTION

Based on the preparation of the two lists, what topics do you believe we should specifically address in this or subsequent team meetings?

IF YOU HAVE MORE TIME

After discussing each item, have team members work in small groups to answer the discussion question above.

Have each small group report its answers to the total group and discuss.

TIPS

Prepare a list of seven "Dos" based on the discussion of the Best list, and distribute printed copies later.

Prepare a list of seven "Don'ts" based on the discussion of the Worst list, and distribute printed copies later.

WHAT'S THE PROBLEM?

Agenda

```
· _____
· _____
· _____
· _____
· _____
· _____
```

OBJECTIVE

To build a meeting agenda out of problems identified by the team.

MATERIALS REQUIRED

Flip chart.

PROCEDURE

Mention that too many meetings may miss the mark because participants never know the expected outcomes or really "buy into" the objectives. To prevent that from happening, explain that you're going to give everyone a chance to help clarify the objectives for this meeting and suggest ways to achieve these objectives.

Set the stage by introducing the meeting topic, e.g., "Our goal this morning is to identify at least a dozen ways we can secure new accounts...." Make certain all attendees have enough background information or experience on the assigned topics.

Give participants 2 minutes to think (individually) about the problem or topic and jot down the major obstacles they can identify that might preclude your reaching the goal.

Ask each participant to name one possible obstacle. Create a list of potential obstacles on a chart pad.

After all reports are made, the listed problems become the agenda, and the balance of the time is spent working on these.

TIP

Remind the group that we tend to identify obstacles outside of ourselves and perhaps neglect to take responsibility for our own problems.

WHAT DO I (WE) WANT IN LIFE?

OBJECTIVES

To identify, and share, team members' values.

To use the values exercise as a laboratory for assessing and improving the team's communication and conflict-resolution skills.

MATERIALS REQUIRED

Copies of the What Are My Values? form; overhead transparency or flip chart with values listed.

PROCEDURE

Provide all team members with a copy of the What Are My Values? form on page 95, and ask them to complete it individually, using column 2. This will serve as the first step in personal goal clarification and goal setting.

To obtain a profile of member responses, display either an overhead transparency or a flip chart with the values listed on it. Ask each participant to state his or her *number one value*. As each person shares the number one value, place a check mark next to that value on the transparency or flip chart so that a group profile emerges.

Discuss the similarities and differences among group members' responses.

DISCUSSION QUESTIONS

1. How does our team mission support our values?
2. How does our team mission conflict with our values?
3. What can we do to reduce the conflicts?
4. How can we as team members work together to create an environment that is respectful of each other's values?

IF YOU HAVE MORE TIME

Ask the team to arrive at a group consensus on the rankings that the typical American would provide. Enter these responses in column 4.

When they have finished, share the key with them (for column 3), and let them compute a measure of their similarity or dissimilarity to other Americans by calculating the sum of the absolute arithmetic differences (without regard to +/− sign) between their individual rankings and the key (enter this difference score in column 1), and between their group rankings and the key (enter this difference score in column 5).

Ask the following questions in addition to the Discussion Questions.

✔ What are the possible reasons for the differences in rankings observed?

✔ What are the implications of your own rankings?

SOURCE

Adapted from Sandra J. Ball-Rokeach, Milton Rokeach, and Joel W. Grube, "The Great American Values Test," *Psychology Today*, November, 1984.

WHAT ARE MY VALUES?

DIRECTIONS: *Examine each of the following items. Rank order them, in column 2, from 1–9 (1 = highest priority; 9 = lowest) according to the priority you would place on achieving them. Later, if small groups are formed, discuss the items with other team members and arrive at a consensus ranking in column 4 for the priority order in which you feel the typical American would rank them.*

VALUE	1 Individual Difference	2 Individual	3 Key	4 Group	5 Group Difference
An exciting life					
A sense of accomplishment					
A world of beauty					
Family security					
Freedom					
Happiness					
Inner harmony					
National security					
True friendship					

TOTALS _____   _____

KEY TO VALUES EXERCISE

VALUE	AMERICANS' RANK
AN EXCITING LIFE	9
A SENSE OF ACCOMPLISHMENT	4
A WORLD OF BEAUTY	8
FAMILY SECURITY	1
FREEDOM	2
HAPPINESS	3
INNER HARMONY	6
NATIONAL SECURITY	7
TRUE FRIENDSHIP	5

PEAK PERFORMANCE

OBJECTIVES

To allow group members to identify a specific activity or incident that was a Peak Performance.

To encourage setting team goals for excellent performance.

MATERIALS REQUIRED

None.

PROCEDURE

In a discussion of excellence or quality service (or other relevant topics), comment that we've all experienced those special moments of a peak performance.

Tell members to think of a peak experience that they are willing to share with the rest of the group.

Ask for volunteers to share their peak experiences. Tell them to limit their comments to 1 minute each.

DISCUSSION QUESTIONS

1. What are the common themes that emerged?
2. How do various people view a peak performance?
3. What can this group do to facilitate a peak performance experience?

TIP

Accumulate industry stories of exceptional customer service. Tell a few stories (e.g., the delivery person who rented a helicopter to get an important package delivered on time) to set the tone for the session.

GOAL SETTING/ ACTION PLANNING

OBJECTIVES

To establish a positive climate and spirit of cooperation among team members.

To develop a team vision and goals.

MATERIALS REQUIRED

Flip charts.

PROCEDURE

Ask group members to spend 2 minutes developing a mental image of what their work situation would ideally be like a year from now.

Ask everyone to describe their visions. Limit comments to 1 minute per person. Post the descriptions on a flip chart.

Enlist or appoint a subgroup that will take the flip charts and, prior to the next meeting, develop a skeletal action plan listing the items directly or indirectly under the full group's control that must be accomplished in the next year to achieve the overall vision. Make presentation and discussion of the action plan an agenda item for the next meeting.

DISCUSSION QUESTIONS

1. How feasible is your overall plan? Will you have achieved your desired objectives a year from now?

2. What factors may prevent you from being successful? (For example: lack of agreement on the goal or plan; lack of resources; unforeseen events.)

3. How often will you review your progress toward the goal?

Don't allow the group to forget their goals and action plans. Distribute sets of them; post them conspicuously; refer to them periodically; check up on progress toward their achievement in both individual interactions and team meetings.

6

How Are We Doing?

Improving Teamwork

THE I'S HAVE IT!

OBJECTIVES

To show that team members tend to be more self-centered than they might realize.

To demonstrate the importance of focusing on other people.

MATERIALS REQUIRED

None.

PROCEDURE

After a discussion on interpersonal skills or any aspect of communication, casually mention that many of us forget about focusing on others and instead become somewhat self-centered, albeit not in a conscious way.

With this in mind, ask the participants to find a partner and for the next 2 minutes, talk about anything in the world they want to discuss. There is, however, one rule: *They cannot use the word "I."* They can do anything else they want; they just can't say "I."

After the 2 minutes (which is usually interspersed with laughter and high energy), call time out and lead the discussion.

DISCUSSION QUESTIONS

1. How many of you were able to talk for those 2 minutes without using the pronoun "I"?
2. Why do so many of us have difficulty avoiding the (over) use of "I" in conversation?
3. How do you feel when talking to (listening to) someone who starts every sentence with "I"?

4. How can we phrase our communications to better focus on the other person?

5. If you did not use the word "I," what strategies did you use to avoid it? Could you do those things more often in your work (or social) environment?

TIP

As an alternative, give each pair the instruction only to talk for 2 minutes. However, instruct one member of each pair to count the number of times "I" is used. The subsequent reports will raise some "I"-brows!

HOW SHARP ARE YOU?

OBJECTIVE

To help team members be alert to tiny details and assumptions that hold the key to success.

MATERIALS REQUIRED

Transparency or handout of the questions on page 109.

PROCEDURE

Present the How Sharp Are You? quiz to the team, setting a very tight time limit (e.g., 3 minutes) for answering the questions.

Before you present the correct answers to them, ask how many had the (most likely) *incorrect* answer for each one (e.g., 13 hours and 45 minutes for #1; 4 [September, April, June, and November] for #2; 11 for #3).

Then present the answers to them, and lead a discussion.

DISCUSSION QUESTIONS

1. What factors caused you to err?
2. How might those factors affect your work performance?
3. What can you do to control such factors?

TIP

Remind team members to read carefully, and to think. Urge them to identify the assumptions they make for each question.

HOW SHARP ARE YOU?

1. Being very tired, a child went to bed at 7:00 o'clock at night. The child had a morning piano lesson, and therefore wound and set the alarm clock to ring at 8:45. How many hours of sleep could the child get before the alarm rings? _____

2. Some months (like October) have 31 days. Only February has precisely 28 (except in a leap year). How many months have 30 days? _____

3. A farmer had 18 pigs, and all but 7 died. How many were left? _____

4. Divide 50 by 1/3, and add 7. What is the answer? _____

5. What is the minimum number of active baseball players on the playing field during any part of an inning? _____ Maximum? _____

6. What 4 words appear on every denomination of U.S. currency? _____ _____ _____ _____

7. If a physician gave you five pills and told you to take one every half-hour, how long would your supply last? _____

8. If you had only one match and entered a cold, dimly lit room where there was a kerosene lamp, an oil heater, and a wood-burning stove, which would you light first? _____

9. Two women play checkers. They play 5 games without a draw game and each woman wins the same number of games. How can this be? _____

10. What word is mispelled in this test? _____

HOW SHARP ARE YOU?

HANDOUT

KEY:

1. 1 hour and 45 minutes.
2. 11 months (all but February).
3. 7 pigs lived.
4. 157 (3 × 50, +7).
5. 10 (9 fielders + 1 batter); 13 (9 + 1 batter + 3 baserunners). Add 1 if you count the on-deck batter.
6. "In God We Trust," or "United States of America."
7. Two hours (now, + 4 half-hours).
8. The match.
9. They aren't playing against each other.
10. "Mispelled" is misspelled.

JOE DOODLEBUG

OBJECTIVES

To encourage participants to explore the assumptions they make when approaching problems.

To encourage participants to learn to ask good questions.

MATERIALS REQUIRED

Copies of the story for each participant. (See page 115.)

PROCEDURE

Present the Joe Doodlebug story to the team. Ask them to work either individually or together to solve the problem. Then lead them in a brief discussion of the exercise.

Hints:

1. Joe does not necessarily have to face the direction he is jumping.
2. Joe could be at any stage of a series of jumps—he might have jumped 1, 2, or 3 times.

Key: Joe appears to have just finished the first in a series of four jumps. He is facing north, but is jumping sideways, moving toward the east. Therefore, he must continue to make three more sideways jumps to the east, and then one large sideways jump back to the west to reach the food.

DISCUSSION QUESTIONS

1. What prevented us as individuals or as a team from solving the problem?

2. What helped us as individuals or as a team to see the light?

3. What does this exercise tell you about the merits of framing a problem (putting it into a larger context; exploring our assumptions and their implications)?

4. How can we learn to identify extraneous information and sort it out?

5. How will this exercise help us as individuals and as a team in the future?

TIP

If the team becomes stuck after a few minutes, ask them to identify a) which way Joe is jumping, and b) which jumps in the series Joe has already taken.

JOE DOODLEBUG STORY

THE SITUATION:

Joe Doodlebug is an imaginary, and somewhat strange, bug. These are his capabilities and limitations in his world:

1. His world is flat.
2. He can only jump (not crawl, fly, walk, roll, or otherwise move across or under the surface of his world).
3. He cannot turn around.
4. He can jump very large distances or very small distances, but not less than one inch per jump nor more than 500 feet per jump.
5. He can jump in only four perfectly true directions—north, south, east, and west. He cannot jump diagonally (e.g., southeast, northwest).
6. He likes to average 15 feet per jump on a good day.
7. There are no other doodlebugs, or other creatures, to help him.
8. Once he starts in any direction, he must jump four times in that same direction before he can switch to another direction.
9. Joe is totally dependent on his owner to provide his food source.

THE PROBLEM:

Joe has been out jumping all over the place while getting some much-needed exercise. As a matter of fact, Joe has worked up a voracious appetite. Much to his pleasure, his owner appears and places a large pile of delectable food 3 feet, 7 inches directly west of him. Joe wants the food, and he wants it fast. As soon as Joe sees all this wonderful food, he stops dead in his tracks (he is facing north). After all his exercise he is very hungry, and even weak. Therefore, he wants to get to the food as quickly as he possibly can, minimizing especially the number of jumps he makes (it's the starting of a jump—the spring required in his legs—that takes the most energy). After briefly surveying the situation, he realizes that *he cannot—at this point—jump due west*. Suddenly he exclaims, "I've got it. I'll only have to jump four times to get to the food!"

YOUR TASK:

Accept the fact that Joe was a smart bug, and dead right in his conclusions. Why did Joe Doodlebug have to take precisely four jumps in order to reach the food with a minimum expenditure of energy? Describe the circumstances that Joe must have been in to reach this conclusion.

115

MORE ON OXYMORONS

OBJECTIVES

To demonstrate the merits of team-work.

To provide a lighthearted opportunity for individuals to vent.

Jumbo shrimp

S... ...erence

Terribly enjoyable

Serious...

Even odds

MATERIALS REQUIRED

A transparency of the master list, and prizes.

PROCEDURE

This can be used either as a quick break during a concentrated meeting, or as a device to draw participants' attention back to the meeting following a refreshment break. It can also be highly effective when it is used almost spontaneously, in response to a participant's unconscious use of an oxymoronic phrase (e.g., "in my unbiased opinion").

Ask the group to identify oxymorons that they are familiar with, and list these on a flip chart.

At the end of the discussion, the master list of oxymorons on page 119 can provide a humorous conclusion.

Prizes can be awarded to those who offer the most creative answers. Alternatively, group competition can be used to see which team generates the largest list in 5 minutes.

DISCUSSION QUESTIONS

1. Why do oxymorons exist?
2. What is your favorite one (or the most frequently heard one in this organization)?
3. What role do oxymorons play in the organization?
4. How does this exercise demonstrate the merits of collective effort?

Make sure that everyone knows what an oxymoron really is (don't assume it is "old news" to them, as they may only vaguely understand oxymorons).

OXYMORONS

Acute dullness

Almost perfect

Bad health

Bittersweet

Blameless culprit

Cardinal sin

Clearly confused

Conservative liberal

Constant variable

Deafening silence

Definite maybe

Deliberately thoughtless

Even odds

Exact estimate

Express mail

Extensive briefing

Freezer burn

Friendly takeover

Genuine imitation

Good grief!

Government efficiency

Holy war

Home office

Idiot savant

Instant classic

Intense apathy

Jumbo shrimp

Justifiably paranoid

Larger half

Least favorite

Linear curve

Liquid gas

Mild interest

Military intelligence

Minor miracle

Modern history

Nonalcoholic beer

Nondairy creamer

Normal deviation

Old news

Only choice

Open secret

Original copies

Passively aggressive

Player coach

Pretty ugly

Qualified success

Randomly organized

Real potential

Rock opera

Rolling stop

Same difference

Silent scream

Simply superb

Sweet sorrow

Taped live

Terribly enjoyable

Tragic comedy

Unbiased opinion

Uncrowned king

Unsung hero

Vaguely aware

Wall Street ethics

War games

Working vacation

SOURCE: *The New York Public Library Desk Reference,* New York: Simon and Schuster, 1989, p. 286.

TOXIC WASTE DUMP

OBJECTIVES

To provide an opportunity for planning and experiencing team-work.

To provide a live forum for analyzing planning prerequisites, processes, and consequences.

To focus the team's attention on how members work together to accomplish objectives.

MATERIALS REQUIRED

Instruction sheet for each participant, 2 coffee cans, enough popcorn kernels to fill one can about halfway, 6–8 pieces of 7½-foot rope, a large sheet of plastic, a rope about 50' long, and 1 bicycle tire tube.

PROCEDURE

Ask the team to identify the characteristics of highly effective teams. Explain that effective teams pay close attention to both the task and the process (i.e., how they work together to accomplish their objective).

Establish an open space for the group, with an 8-foot di-ameter circle marked off with rope.

Distribute the instruction sheet (see page 123) to each person, and start the clock running.

Enforce the rules very strictly.

DISCUSSION QUESTIONS

1. Was your team successful? By what measures?

2. What did your team do that helped it succeed?

3. What did your team members do that caused it problems?

4. What did you learn from this exercise that you can apply on the job?

TIP

Select a larger (green) can for the safe one; a smaller (red) can for the toxic one.

Note to Team Leaders: Most groups accomplish this (after due discussion and planning) by folding over the tire tube into a smaller circle, tying 3–5 short ropes to various sides of it, and stretching it to fit over (and grab) the toxic can. By coordinating their efforts, one member slides around the circle with his or her rope to become the controller of the dumping process while the others hold the can suspended above the safe can. Through delicate maneuvers, they can accomplish the task. The plastic sheet underneath the circle and cans makes cleanup much easier when they spill, however.

TOXIC WASTE DUMP: INSTRUCTIONS

SETTING

A can of highly toxic popcorn has contaminated a circle approximately 8 feet in diameter. The toxic area extends to the ceiling. If the poisonous popcorn is not transferred to a safe container for decontamination, the toxic popcorn will contaminate and destroy the population of the entire city. The popcorn is estimated to have a safe life of exactly 30 minutes before it explodes. Obviously, there is insufficient time to contact authorities and evacuate the city. Therefore, the lives of thousands of people are in your hands.

Inside the circle you will find two cans. One (unsafe) container is about half full of the toxic popcorn. The other (safe) container is available for decontamination.

TEAM GOAL

You must find a way to safely transfer the toxic popcorn from the unsafe container to the safe container, using only the materials provided to you. For your group, this includes a piece of rope (each approximately 7½ feet long) for each person, and a bicycle tire tube.

RULES

1. **No** member may cross the plane of the circle with any part of the body. If this occurs, they must be taken to the hospital immediately (removed from play) and they may not participate in any form from then on. The group is responsible for the safety of all its members.

2. **No** member may sacrifice himself or herself to aid in the transfer of the popcorn.

3. **No** spills are allowed, or the popcorn will explode.

4. Members may **only** use the materials provided. However, they can be used in any way desired.

5. The popcorn will not spread its toxicity to the safe can, the ropes, the tube, or the instruction-giver. The members have **no** protection inside the imaginary cylinder created by the 8-foot diameter circle.

6. The safe container may move anywhere in or outside of the circle. The unsafe container must stay *inside* the circle, and not be moved more than one foot from its center.

7. Remember, the popcorn *must* be transferred within 30 minutes, or there will be a tremendous disaster.

IS IT A "GO" OR "NO GO"?

OBJECTIVE

To help a facilitator discover whether there is truly consensus among team members.

MATERIALS REQUIRED

An adequate supply of signal cards.

PROCEDURE

This procedure helps to combat one of the greatest dangers in team decision making—the false assumption that a consensus has been reached because "no one spoke up." You *need* to know whether the team supports ("go") or does not support ("no go") a proposal before proceeding with it.

Before the lesson, create signal cards that can be used to send nonverbal messages from members to you. One option is to obtain poster boards that are, say, red on one side and green on the other. Cut them up into 3-inch squares.

At the beginning of the session, distribute one square of each color to each participant.

Ask them to display a colored card—either continuously or periodically in response to direct questions. The green cards should be displayed when they agree with an emerging conclusion (or pace of discussion). The red cards should be shown when they are opposed to a proposed action or are dissatisfied with the pace or direction of discussion. You may want to provide additional cards for other signals—such as white for neutrality or yellow for uncertainty.

DISCUSSION QUESTIONS

1. What is the meaning of *consensus*?

2. How important is it to discover what others are thinking and feeling?

3. What responsibility do we have for soliciting this information? For acting on it?

IF YOU HAVE MORE TIME

You might also consider creating sets of Olympic-style judging cards (e.g., 10, 9, 8, ...) for each member. Then, in response to a question that probes for the degree of agreement or support, you can obtain a quick assessment of the *potency* of their feelings.

TIPS

It will likely take a few reminders for the group to become familiar with and willing to use this procedure. However, they will soon remember to display the proper card if you call on someone to explain their concerns and they discover that they have mistakenly left their red card on display.

The key is to use the procedure regularly, and not just on rare occasions. It can be a highly effective way for the facilitator to obtain either subtle or not-so-subtle cues from the team about their reactions to a topic or progress on it.

Think carefully about the form of the questions you plan to ask. The "cleanest" ones have a yes/no or true/false or agree/disagree response pattern to them.

Remind the team that the signal cards are not just for your benefit. They, too, can look around the room to find out what others are thinking.

ZAP! YOU'RE A GROUP!

OBJECTIVES

To speed the development of working groups into teams.

To demonstrate issues related to group dynamics, team building, problem solving, time management, organization, and leadership under a severe time constraint.

MATERIALS REQUIRED

Flip chart and felt-tip pens.

Optional: A written statement of a work problem and its background.

PROCEDURE

Divide the group into subgroups of 3 to 4 persons.

Announce that the team is to work on a specific task for the next 6 minutes. At the end of the time period, a representative needs to present a written flip chart summarizing the team's conclusions. The presentation is limited to 1 minute.

Present the team with a task of your choice, preferably one that is organizationally relevant or job related. (An example might be, "Brainstorm various ways to reduce the turnover in our company by 10% within the next 90 days," or, "Suggest ways in which we could substantially improve customer service.")

Answer any procedural questions they may have, then walk away (to a place where you can observe and listen, but not interact).

DISCUSSION QUESTIONS

1. Who emerged as the leader? Why?

2. Who played what other roles within the group? What other roles needed to be played but received low priority?

3. What problems did the group encounter? How were they overcome? How could they be handled differently?

4. What was the effect of severe time pressure on the group's motivation? On its ultimate productivity? What about the absence (nonparticipation) of the formal leader of the full team?

TIPS

Make sure you have an engaging task for the group—one they can easily understand and identify with as significant.

Remind the team of the importance of playing a variety of roles as the situation calls for—questioning, summarizing, seeking and giving relevant information, encouraging, etc.

7

How Can We Stretch Our Minds?

Problem-Solving and Creativity Games

CREATIVE PEOPLE I HAVE KNOWN

OBJECTIVES

To identify traits of creative people.

To illustrate the point that these same characteristics are often common to everyone.

MATERIALS REQUIRED

None.

PROCEDURE

Ask the group members to think of some friends or colleagues who they consider to be creative people. (In the event that participants seem to have difficulty identifying acquaintances, it is acceptable to list other well-known creative people, e.g., Walt Disney.)

Have them write down the names of 4–5 people that fit that category, and then, next to the name of each person, write out what that particular person *has* or *does* that makes him or her creative. These responses could include such things as "always asking questions" or "always willing to take a risk" or "daydreams a lot."

Following this individual activity, form groups of 4–5 participants to compare and contrast the names and qualities of creative people.

DISCUSSION QUESTIONS

1. What are some of the traits or qualities your friends or colleagues exhibit that make them creative? Could you learn these qualities?

2. In your organization, have you seen cases where colleagues show creativity even though the job climate does not seem to foster creativity?

3. How does one become creative in a climate that doesn't currently support creativity?

TIP

To support the theme in question 1, ask the team to assess each item in the list of characteristics according to whether it is a genetic trait or a behavior. Most will be behaviors, implying that they can be taught, learned, and applied by many.

CREATIVITY NOT SPOKEN HERE

OBJECTIVES

To uncover several obstacles to creativity that are prevalent in many organizations.

To suggest ways of overcoming obstacles to creativity.

MATERIALS REQUIRED

Flip chart and markers.

PROCEDURE

After discussing some elements of creativity (behavioral examples, etc.), acknowledge that in some organizations, creativity is sometimes purposely or inadvertently blocked by policy, people, or the overall culture.

Ask the group to form subgroups of 3–4 people and discuss this question:

Why aren't we (or others) as creative as we (they) either could be or should be?

Allow 3 minutes for groups to think up as many reasons as they can. Responses will likely include such things as:

Boss	Job climate
No time	Past experience
Lack of skill	Laziness

After 3–4 minutes, ask each group to appoint a spokesperson and identify just a few of their roadblocks. Have a volunteer record these on a flip chart or chalkboard.

After most ideas have been captured, ask each group to go through its own list and identify which of the items listed actually are under their own control as opposed to the control of others.

DISCUSSION QUESTIONS

1. Were you surprised to see such a long list?
2. Did some of these items hit close to home?
3. For those items listed for which you have some control, how can you overcome those obstacles?
4. For those over which you have no control (boss, policy, etc.), how can you lessen their impact?

TIP

Point out that drawing upon a group for intellectual aid is already a form of creativity—or at least a substitute for individual creativity!

IDEA-SPURRING QUESTIONS

OBJECTIVE

To be used in creativity sessions to encourage more ideas, adaptations, and innovations.

MATERIALS REQUIRED

Copies of the Idea-Spurring Questions.

PROCEDURE

After introductory comments on the need for continuing improvement in all segments of any organization, pass out copies of the handout appearing on page 137.

Give the group a couple of minutes to read through the sheet and then call their attention to the first question, "Who." Ask them to provide examples they have experienced personally that illustrate one of these points, or an example they can recall in a general way.

Continue on to the second point, "What," and repeat the discussion, eliciting 4–5 responses of real-world examples.

Proceed through the remaining questions, allowing ample time for participant examples.

DISCUSSION QUESTIONS

1. How can these questions help you in problem solving and innovation?
2. Which set of questions do you find yourself using most often?
3. Which question is the most thought-provoking?
4. What other useful questions have you heard that should be added to the list?

To initiate the exercise, read the Rudyard Kipling poem, "Six Honest Serving Men," from *The Elephant's Child*:

I keep six honest serving men
(They taught me all I knew);
Their names are What and Why and When
and How and Where and Who.

IDEA-SPURRING QUESTIONS

HANDOUT

Emerson has stated that "the ability to create is the ability to adapt." Here are some items that can be used as a springboard for other ideas. Change, adapt, add, or delete as necessary.

1. WHO
- ✔ Who can help or make contributions?
- ✔ Who must I "sell" on this idea?
- ✔ Who can help me get additional resources?
- ✔ Who will benefit?

2. WHAT
- ✔ What do I need by way of additional resources?
- ✔ What techniques or methods can I use?
- ✔ What is the best way? The first step?
- ✔ What will make the idea better?

3. WHERE
- ✔ Where should I start?
- ✔ Where is resistance likely to be found?
- ✔ Where should I "plant seeds"?

4. WHEN
- ✔ When should I introduce the plan?
- ✔ When should we implement the ideas?
- ✔ When should we revise our strategy?

5. WHY
- ✔ Why should they buy this idea?
- ✔ Why is this way better?
- ✔ Why is the resistance so strong?

6. HOW
- ✔ How can we improve on the idea?
- ✔ How can we "test the waters"?
- ✔ How can I persuade centers of influence?

PIPE DREAMS

OBJECTIVES

To stimulate team members to practice creativity during a group meeting.

To allow individuals to give themselves permission to be creative.

MATERIALS REQUIRED

Sufficient pipe cleaners (3 per person); prizes.

PROCEDURE

Before the meeting begins, place 3 pipe cleaners at each person's place. Unless someone asks what they are for, do not tell them their use until you are halfway through the meeting.

At that time, tell the team that these items are theirs to make any kind of a personalized sculpture. If asked further, simply restate they can do anything they want with them. (Urge them to be creative.)

At the end of the meeting, ask the team to select a winner.

Note: Give special recognition to any members who combined their "resources" (i.e., pipe cleaners), and designed or built something that uses all their tools. Also, mention that children typically don't wait to ask, they simply go ahead with the task.

Provide small prizes for the winners.

DISCUSSION QUESTIONS

1. How many were curious when they saw these pipe cleaners?

2. Why didn't you ask their purpose?

3. Why did you wait to be told what to do with them?

4. How many of you opted to approach this task as a team? Who initiated this idea with your group?

TIP

Bring a Polaroid-type camera and take close-up photos of the winners and their products. Tape these to a poster board for a strong visual reminder of creativity within the team.

PLEASE PASS THE PROBLEMS

OBJECTIVE

To obtain several possible solutions or suggestions for the participants' current challenges or problems.

MATERIALS REQUIRED

Paper, notepads, and pencils.

PROCEDURE

The team should be sitting around a table or in a circle.

Ask each person to think about a current job-related problem or concern.

Each person writes his or her problem on a blank sheet of paper or on a notepad. Examples might be, "How can I get more group involvement?" or, "How can I get my staff to be more punctual?" After allowing a few minutes to think about and write out their problems, ask each person to pass his or her problem sheet to the right. That person reads the problem just received and jots down the first thought(s) that come to mind for addressing that problem. Allow 30 seconds to respond to that individual sheet.

Repeat this rotational process every 30 seconds, and keep the process going until each person gets his or her own sheet back.

Time permitting, they can then discuss some of the more practical solutions they have received.

DISCUSSION QUESTIONS

1. Did anyone discover novel solutions that you had not previously considered?

2. Can you see any value in trying some of these suggestions?

3. Do some of these suggestions trigger other ideas or solutions for you?

4. What lesson does this teach us about reaching out to others for their assistance?

TIP

Encourage individuals, as they formulate their problem statements, to frame them in a way that stimulates and allows the greatest creativity by respondents (and simultaneously avoids limiting their problem-solving processes).

THE PROBLEM-SOLVING WHEEL

OBJECTIVE

To secure possible solutions for participants' questions, concerns, or problems.

MATERIALS REQUIRED

Room with movable chairs or some setup that allows for rearrangement.

PROCEDURE

Arrange the room so that chairs can be placed in circular fashion with five chairs encircling (and facing) five other chairs (double circles, with chairs pointing at each other). The five persons seated in each chair of the outer ring will be "consultants" to those in the inner circle who are "clients."

The client explains an important question or problem to the consultant for 1 minute. The consultant has 2 minutes to discuss, clarify, offer suggestions, etc.

After the 3-minute mark (total), the consultant moves to his or her left. Now the participants in the outer and inner rings will reverse roles, with each person in the outer ring becoming a client of the counterpart in the inner ring. The client has 1 minute to state the problem and the consultant has 2 minutes to respond.

DISCUSSION QUESTIONS

1. How many of you received some solid, usable answers?
2. Will some of you share your stories?
3. Why is it that many of us have no reservations about telling our problems to total strangers?

4. What kinds of consultant skills were most effective in helping you open up and making you receptive to their solutions?

IF YOU HAVE MORE TIME

After the 3-minute mark (total), the consultant moves to his or her left and repeats the process with a new client who poses the same question or problem to the new consultant.

Repeat this process with the 3-minute time limit.

Continue for 3 more rounds and then have the members change to the other circle. (Clients move to the outside circle where they will now be consultants.)

Repeat the entire sequence as time allows.

TIP

Provide clients with a note sheet on which they can record the highlights of the solutions they heard. (There is little so frustrating as a solid solution that is later forgotten!)

MANAGERIAL LITERACY: THE ACRONYM TEST

OBJECTIVES

To give team members the opportunity to demonstrate, individually or collectively, their familiarity with common business acronyms.

To demonstrate the benefits of collective effort on a task.

MATERIALS NEEDED

Sufficient copies of the test for each participant; a transparency of the key; prizes.

PROCEDURE

Distribute copies of the Managerial Literacy test to each member. Choose 3 team members to collaborate on the test. The others will work individually.

Allow everyone a reasonable but limited amount of time to work on the test. (An alternative is to distribute it just before a break and let them work on it as a social mixer. You can also distribute it at the end of a meeting and ask everyone to bring the completed test to the next meeting. A third alternative is to send it to them in advance of the meeting along with other advance readings.)

If you wish, the individuals and the team of 3 may score themselves by examining the key you will display.

Then call for a show of hands to identify who got 0–10 correct, 11–20 correct, 21–30 correct, etc.

Lead the group in applauding the high-scoring individuals, possibly providing a small prize (e.g., candy bar, apple, or soft drink) to the top-scoring individual or team.

DISCUSSION QUESTIONS

1. How pervasive is the use of acronyms as a special language in the business world?
2. What are some of the acronyms that are unique to your organization and industry?
3. What are the dysfunctional aspects of using acronyms in everyday language?
4. Did the group of 3 persons outscore the team members who were working alone? Why or why not?

TIP

To save time and also extend the benefit across several teams or sessions, divide the list into smaller tests of 10 to 25 items.

SOURCE

Adapted from Gary Shaw and Jack Weber, *Managerial Literacy: What Today's Managers Must Know to Succeed*, Homewood, Illinois: Dow Jones-Irwin, 1990.

146

MANAGERIAL LITERACY TEST

DIRECTIONS: *Identify these acronyms:*

1. AFL-CIO
2. AI
3. AMEX
4. AP & AR
5. BARS
6. BCG matrix
7. CAD-CAM
8. CAPM
9. CBOE
10. CBT
11. CD
12. CEO
13. CFA
14. CFO
15. CI
16. COGS
17. COO
18. CPA
19. CPI
20. CPU
21. CRP
22. DJIA
23. DP
24. EBIT
25. ECU

26. EEC
27. EEOC
28. EFT
29. EOQ
30. EPA
31. EPS
32. ESOP
33. FASB
34. FAX
35. FDIC
36. FICA
37. FIFO
38. FOB
39. FSLIC
40. FTC
41. FY
42. GAAP
43. GATT
44. GDP
45. GNP
46. HMO
47. HRM
48. IMF
49. IPO
50. IRR

51. IRS
52. ISDN
53. IT
54. JIT
55. LAN
56. LBO
57. LDC
58. LIFO
59. MBA
60. MBO
61. MBWA
62. MIS
63. MITI
64. MLP
65. MNC
66. MRP
67. NASDAQS
68. NLRA
69. NLRB
70. NPV
71. NYSE
72. OD
73. OPEC
74. OPIC
75. OR

76. OSHA
77. OTC
78. P&L
79. P,P,&E
80. P/E
81. PAC
82. PC
83. PERT
84. PIMS
85. PLC
86. PPI
87. PR
88. QWL
89. R&D
90. RFP
91. ROA
92. ROE
93. ROI
94. S&P
95. SBU
96. SEC
97. SMSA
98. TQM
99. UAW
100. VAT

1. AFL-CIO—American Federation of Labor-Congress of Ind. Organizations
2. AI—Artificial Intelligence
3. AMEX—AMerican (stock) EXchange
4. AP & AR—Accounts Payable and Accounts Receivable
5. BARS—Behaviorally-Anchored Rating Scale
6. BCG matrix—Boston Consulting Group matrix
7. CAD-CAM—Computer-Aided Design/Computer-Aided Manufacturing
8. CAPM—Capital Asset Pricing Model
9. CBOE—Chicago Board Options Exchange
10. CBT—Chicago Board of Trade
11. CD—Certificate of Deposit
12. CEO—Chief Executive Officer
13. CFA—Chartered Financial Analyst
14. CFO—Chief Financial Officer
15. CI—Continuous Improvement
16. COGS—Cost of Goods Sold
17. COO—Chief Operating Officer
18. CPA—Certified Public Accountant
19. CPI—Consumer Price Index
20. CPU—Central Processing Unit
21. CRP—Capacity Requirements Planning
22. DJIA—Dow Jones Industrial Average
23. DP—Data Processing
24. EBIT—Earnings Before Income Taxes
25. ECU—European Currency Unit
26. EEC—European Economic Community
27. EEOC—Equal Employment Opportunity Commission
28. EFT—Electronic Funds Transfer
29. EOQ—Economic Order Quantity
30. EPA—Environmental Protection Agency
31. EPS—Earnings Per Share
32. ESOP—Employee Stock Ownership Plan
33. FASB—Financial Accounting Standards Board
34. FAX—Facsimile
35. FDIC—Federal Deposit Insurance Corporation
36. FICA—Federal Insurance Contributions Act
37. FIFO—First In, First Out
38. FOB—Free On Board
39. FSLIC—Federal Savings & Loan Insurance Corporation
40. FTC—Federal Trade Commission
41. FY—Fiscal Year
42. GAAP—Generally Accepted Accounting Principles
43. GATT—General Agreement on Tariffs and Trade
44. GDP—Gross Domestic Product
45. GNP—Gross National Product
46. HMO—Health Maintenance Organization
47. HRM—Human Resource Management
48. IMF—International Monetary Fund
49. IPO—Initial Public Offering
50. IRR—Internal Rate of Return
51. IRS—Internal Revenue Service
52. ISDN—Integrated Services Digital Network
53. IT—Information Technology
54. JIT—Just In Time
55. LAN—Local Area Network
56. LBO—Leveraged Buy-Out
57. LDC—Less Developed Country
58. LIFO—Last In, First Out
59. MBA—Master of Business Administration
60. MBO—Management by Objectives
61. MBWA—Management by Wandering Around
62. MIS—Management Information Systems
63. MITI—Ministry of International Trade and Industry
64. MLP—Master Limited Partnership
65. MNC—MultiNational Corporation
66. MRP—Materials Requirements Planning
67. NASDAQS—Nat'l. Assoc. of Secur. Dealers Automated Quotation System
68. NLRA—National Labor Relations Act
69. NLRB—National Labor Relations Board
70. NPV—Net Present Value
71. NYSE—New York Stock Exchange
72. OD—Organizational Development
73. OPEC—Organization of Petroleum Exporting Countries
74. OPIC—Overseas Private Investment Corporation
75. OR—Operations Research
76. OSHA—Occupational Safety & Health Act/Administration
77. OTC—Over the Counter
78. P&L—Profit and Loss
79. P,P,&E—Property, Plant, & Equipment
80. P/E—Price/Earnings Ratio
81. PAC—Political Action Committee
82. PC—Personal Computer
83. PERT—Program Evaluation & Review Technique
84. PIMS—Profit Impact of Marketing Strategy
85. PLC—Product Life Cycle
86. PPI—Producer Price Index
87. PR—Public Relations
88. QWL—Quality of Work Life
89. R&D—Research & Development
90. RFP—Request for Proposals
91. ROA—Return on Assets
92. ROE—Return on Equity
93. ROI—Return on Investment
94. S&P—Standard & Poor's
95. SBU—Strategic Business Unit
96. SEC—Securities and Exchange Commission
97. SMSA—Standard Metropolitan Statistical Area
98. TQM—Total Quality Management
99. UAW—United Auto Workers
100. VAT—Value-Added Tax

PLAYING WITH MATCHES

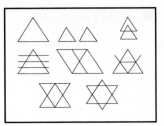

OBJECTIVE

To allow participants to practice creativity during a group meeting.

To provide a warm-up exercise or an opportunity for a change of pace to a group of participants.

MATERIALS REQUIRED

A supply of 6 matches, or equal-length sticks, for each participant. Also a transparency of the key to expedite explanation and illustration to the participants upon completion of the exercise; prizes.

PROCEDURE

Distribute a supply of 6 match sticks to each member of the total group. Ask each person to arrange the sticks in a configuration such that they create (progressively):

✔ one equilateral triangle

✔ two equilateral triangles

✔ three equilateral triangles

✔ four equilateral triangles

✔ six equilateral triangles

✔ eight equilateral triangles

Then ask a volunteer to come forward and demonstrate to the entire group the solution to each task. Provide praise or a small reward to each successful person. Lead the group in a discussion of the work-related implications of engaging in a task such as this.

DISCUSSION QUESTIONS

1. Who was able to complete all the figures?

2. What useful guidelines could be shared with participants to help them in this task?

3. What are the impediments to being able to do this task? (What limitations do we place upon ourselves? How can we remove or prevent these?)

TIP

Some people are skilled at "seeing" geometric shapes and will complete each task quickly. Invite them to use their spare time to generate useful creativity guidelines they will later share with others. Gather and post these after each task, as a way to help others.

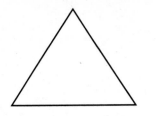

One triangle (with another one super-imposed over it.)

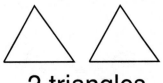

2 triangles

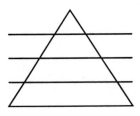

4 triangles

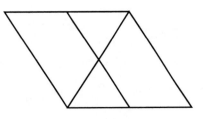

4 triangles (alternate)

6 triangles

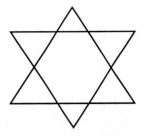

8 triangles

8

Can We Get Along Better?

Learning to Communicate and Cooperate

GIVING AND GETTING

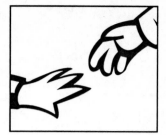

OBJECTIVE

To encourage participants to "reach out and help" other team members whenever necessary.

MATERIALS REQUIRED

None.

PROCEDURE

Ask for a loan of one dollar from a member of the group. Displaying it prominently in one hand, proceed to ask for the loan of a second dollar from another member. Then carefully repay the first loaner with the second dollar, and repay the second loaner with the first dollar. Then ask the rhetorical question, "Is either of these persons now richer than before the exchange?" (Neither is, of course.)

Then point out to the team that, by contrast, had two *ideas* been shared as readily, their respective givers would be richer in experience than they were before. In addition, of course, even the rest of us (bystanders) might be richer.

DISCUSSION QUESTIONS

1. What factors seem to *prevent* us from sharing useful ideas and insights with other group members?
2. What factors should *encourage* us to share ideas and advice with others on a regular basis?
3. What are the underlying behavioral reasons *why* we should aid others (e.g., the law of reciprocity, mutual dependency and expected mutual benefit)?

IF YOU HAVE MORE TIME

Give each participant one or more pieces of preprinted play money (with a blank back side). Let them exchange the money with each other first to experience the lack of enrichment that ensues. Then ask each person to write at least one idea on the play money and give it to another person.

TIP

It is wise to pick a generic problem for the group to focus on. Then, when ideas are generated, almost everyone can gain from them and be "richer."

THE GREAT GLOSSARY SEARCH

OBJECTIVE

To use teamwork to help team members become familiar with new job-related terms.

MATERIALS REQUIRED

List of unfamiliar terms that the team would benefit from knowing—for example, new products, companies, or services in the industry, new technical or management jargon, important client or customer names, etc.

PROCEDURE

Distribute a list of key terms at a team meeting.

Ask members to collaborate with each other to obtain accurate descriptions of the terms by a given deadline, e.g., the next meeting. (Make sure that it is *possible* for the descriptions to be found!)

You may also choose to drop hints about where the terms may be located, or you might willingly engage in breaktime or on-the-job discussions that help clarify the terms.

Help the team decide how to delegate portions of the task to each member while encouraging collaboration. Set aside time at the next meeting to determine how the team did.

DISCUSSION QUESTIONS

1. Which terms were most difficult to identify?
2. What additional sources did you contact to complete the task?
3. How many of you teamed together to define some terms? Did this help?

4. How will this task, featuring independent responsibility and active learning, help you to retain an understanding of these terms in the future?

TIP

This game works best when each member has somewhat unique knowledge to share (e.g., a project team drawn from a matrix structure). It also works well when a major change effort (e.g, reengineering) with new terms is being introduced into the organization.

TEAM CHARADES

OBJECTIVE

To establish a group identity and high level of cohesiveness in a work team.

MATERIALS REQUIRED

None.

PROCEDURE

Divide the team into 2 groups for a team-naming competition.

Ask each group to choose a name for the team that best identifies it—one to which they could easily relate.

Call upon each group to act out (mime) its name in charades fashion, while the group tries to guess the name of the group that is on stage.

Have the combined team, working together, decide which name best identifies the team and explain why.

DISCUSSION QUESTIONS

1. How did your group select its name?
2. How comfortable are all of you with it?
3. How important is it to have a group identity?

TIP

An engaging follow-up step is to ask the team to develop, and then demonstrate, a group cheer they will commit to using every time they succeed at something (e.g., celebrating small wins such as gaining a new customer).

DEPARTMENT X-Y-Z

CPD
(Counter-Productivity Development)

PHDS
(Productivity and Human Design System)

WIND
(Widely Implemented Managerial Decisionmaking

OBJECTIVES

To build a spirit of teamwork.

To practice creativity.

To practice informal speaking skills.

MATERIALS REQUIRED

3 × 5 cards.

PROCEDURE

Break the team into subgroups of about 5 people each.

Give each subgroup a card with a nonsensical acronym (3–4 letters) printed on it and the task of using it to develop a new name for the team.

The subgroup then brainstorms and decides what the letters might stand for and describes to the total team the name of their new department. An example could be PHDS. The team might create Productivity and Human Design Systems and then go on and report the activities and scope of this mythical department. (Allow several minutes for brainstorming and 1–2 minutes for each team report.)

DISCUSSION QUESTIONS

1. What other names did your group consider?
2. How did the group make its selection?
3. In what ways does your team's new name open up opportunities? In what ways does it limit its flexibility?

163

In addition to having each team describe its new name, have them do the following: Explain this mythical department's objectives, describe its scope, and report on its typical activities. (Allow 8–10 minutes for brainstorming and 3–4 minutes for each team report.) A panel could be named to select the winning team.

TIPS

Let the group select the most creative team name, and award a prize to its members.

I WISH, I WISH ...

OBJECTIVE

To determine real problem areas in a team or organization.

MATERIALS REQUIRED

3 × 5 cards.

PROCEDURE

At a team meeting, point out the importance of periodically checking on the levels of team cohesiveness, cooperation, and member satisfaction. Tell members that the next activity will be one of those periodic check-ups.

Distribute 3 × 5 cards and ask members to write their answers to the questions you will ask. There is no need to sign names. You will collect the cards, review them, synthesize the information, and report the results at the next meeting. Alternatively, ask for a volunteer to collect the cards, synthesize the information, and report at the next meeting.

Ask the following question: "If you could change anything about the team's mission or way of operating, or anything about your role on the team, what would be on your wish list?" Encourage team members to be honest and point out that all comments on the cards are anonymous.

DISCUSSION QUESTIONS

1. What do you like best about your roles and functions on our team? About your job?
2. If you were king or queen for a day, what would you change about the team? In the organization (your job, your office, etc.)?

3. What could we do to make your job better (easier, more fun, etc.)?
4. What would your boss (e.g., team leader) answer as his or her wish?
5. What would your teammates have on their wish lists?
6. What prevents us from making these changes?
7. What might be the potential gains from these changes?

IF YOU HAVE MORE TIME

Schedule personal interviews with team members or people who depend on the team's output, such as internal or external customers or suppliers. Ask the following question: "If you could change anything about the team's mission or way of operating, or anything about your role on the team, what would be on your wish list?"

Share the results of the survey with the team, without attributing specific comments to any particular individual.

As a team, discuss items on the collective wish list. Decide which suggestions to implement and by when.

TIP

You must be willing to feed back to the team a summary of the input they've given, and your decisions as to how to resolve the problems they've raised.

KNOW YOUR DICTIONARY!

1	=	S
2	=	P
3	=	T
4	=	M
5	=	W
6	=	O
7	=	J
8	=	Q
9	=	Z
10	=	X

OBJECTIVE

To demonstrate that there is often substantial benefit from collaborating in small groups to obtain the answers to certain types of questions.

MATERIALS REQUIRED

None, although worksheets for the individual and group rankings and an overhead transparency or flip chart with the answer key could be prepared in advance.

PROCEDURE

Explain that dictionaries, with their hundreds of thousands of entries, contain sharply different numbers of words beginning with each letter in the alphabet. The task today is to identify which of 10 letters is more or less frequently used to begin those words.

Assign half of the team to work in groups of 4 to 5 persons. Tell the other half of the team to do the exercise as individuals. The task for both those working in teams and those working as individuals is to rank order from 1 to 10 the following letters, with 1 designated as the most frequently-used letter to begin words, 2 as the next most frequently used, etc.: O, X, M, S, Z, P, J, T, Q, W. The people assigned to teams are to collaborate on their answers. The people working as individuals may not seek any help. Tell them they have 5 minutes.

When 5 minutes have elapsed, call time. Give the correct answers, or display a copy of the key (correct ranking), as found on page 171. Tell them they can score themselves by assigning an absolute value (without regard to plus or minus sign) to the arithmetic difference between their rank for each letter and the correct rank, and totaling that set of 10 numbers.

Ask those who worked individually to give their scores (the absolute value). Post each score on a flip chart, and compute the average.

Ask each group to give its group score, and post that information. Then compute the average score for the groups.

Lead a discussion about the differences between individual and group scores and possible reasons for the differences in performance.

DISCUSSION QUESTIONS

1. What specific behaviors or actions within each group helped it to perform well or poorly?
2. On what type of tasks do groups perform better than individuals?

IF YOU HAVE MORE TIME

Conduct the activity in two stages.

First, have everyone do the exercise individually, rank ordering from 1 to 10 the following letters, with 1 designated as the most frequently used letter to begin words, 2 as the next most frequently used, etc.: O, X, M, S, Z, P, J, T, Q, W.

Second, after everyone has completed his or her individual ranking, form small groups of 3–5 persons. Working collaboratively, have them rank order the same 10 letters through the use of the collective wisdom in their group.

Now have them score both themselves as individuals, and their groups, by computing the absolute arithmetic difference between their ranking and the key for each letter and totaling that set of 10 numbers.

Add the following question to the Discussion Questions:

How many persons had a group score better than their individual score?

The approximate time required for this version of the activity is 30–40 minutes, plus discussion time.

TIP

If the groups performed better, probe why this was so. Remind them that it isn't simply because of more brainpower, but also due to the willingness of some members to share their knowledge and communicate their insights persuasively.

SOURCE

Webster's *International Dictionary.*

1 = S
2 = P
3 = T
4 = M
5 = W
6 = O
7 = J
8 = Q
9 = Z
10 = X

SCAVENGER HUNT

OBJECTIVE

To quickly immerse group members into a task-oriented activity so they can begin developing a team identity and initial cohesiveness.

MATERIALS REQUIRED

A previously developed list of items (note that the number of copies provided—one or more—to the team might also serve as a contributing factor to various team approaches).

PROCEDURE

Give the team a specific time period for completing the task, and a minimal set of rules to follow (e.g., they must stay within certain physical boundaries).

Provide them with a comprehensive list of objects to obtain (for example: a 1969 penny, a clover blossom, a live ant, a roll of bath tissue, an automobile license plate, a dollar bill with a full-house poker hand represented in the serial number, etc.). It is best to include items that are feasible to obtain, but that may require either ingenuity or collaborative effort within the team to accomplish.

Score the team based on the number of items obtained, and possibly award them with a prize.

DISCUSSION QUESTIONS

1. How did the team organize to conduct its task (e.g., with individuals assigned to specific items, or as pairs, or with everybody trying to do everything)?

2. How was this method chosen (e.g., we thought it over and decided it was best, or we just jumped in and began the task)?

3. How successful was it?

4. What will you do differently when you are now assigned a more serious work task as a team?

TIP

This exercise works best when it is desirable for the team to prepare for later meaningful task assignments, and when it is obvious that participants would benefit from "loosening up."

9

Can We Work Together?

Energizing Team Meetings

POKER-FACED PARTICIPATION

OBJECTIVE

To stimulate a higher level, and a broader distribution, of member participation in the team's discussions.

MATERIALS REQUIRED

A deck of playing cards.

PROCEDURE

Some people are reluctant to get involved in open discussions, especially if they are new members, face a complex or threatening issue, or don't feel comfortable with the leader yet. You can break the ice quickly and stimulate broader (even competitive) group participation in response to your questions by following this method:

✔ Inform the team that they will have the opportunity to play one hand of poker at the end of the meeting. The person with the best overall poker hand will win a prize.

✔ Give one card to each person every time they make a meaningful contribution to the discussion.

✔ At the end of the session, clarify the winning order of poker hands (i.e., royal flush, straight flush, four of a kind, full house, flush, straight, three of a kind, two pair, one pair). Then identify the best five-card hand in the group and award a prize.

DISCUSSION QUESTIONS

1. What impact did this technique have on your *participation*?

2. What carryover impact will it have on your participation in *subsequent* meetings?

3. Did this aid or interfere with your *learning* about the day's discussion topic?

IF YOU HAVE MORE TIME

This game also works well with small groups. Form teams of 3 to 5 persons in advance, and award cards as before. Then give the teams 2 minutes at the end of discussion to pool their resources and form the best poker hand they can. Be sure to have a prize that the *team* can share (e.g., a six-pack of soda)!

HOW DID THIS MEETING GO?

OBJECTIVE

To encourage honest feedback from team members at the conclusion of a meeting or discussion.

MATERIALS REQUIRED

2 flip charts and several colored markers.

PROCEDURE

Place 2 flip charts at the front of the room.

✔ On the first, write: "Here are some things we especially valued about the way the meeting was run today."

✔ On the second, write: "Here are some suggestions as to how future meetings like this could be even better."

Invite participants to spend the next 6 to 8 minutes processing the meeting (consciously reflecting on it and examining both what went well and what merits improvement). Record the essence of all ideas.

Tear off the flip charts and return to your office. You may choose to type up the comments and distribute them to the team members, or you may simply study them yourself to identify any relevant themes or constructive comments affecting things within your control. Then celebrate your success, and change something needing improvement!

DISCUSSION QUESTIONS

1. Which items is there agreement on?

2. Which items is there disagreement on? How can that disagreement be resolved to the relative satisfaction of all concerned?

3. What actions can individual members commit to engaging in to improve meeting effectiveness?

IF YOU HAVE MORE TIME

After identifying what went well and what needs improvement, ask the group to convert those comments into specific, *action-oriented implications*. What new behaviors would they recommend for both you and themselves that would improve the effectiveness of future meetings?

TIP

If the trust level between you and the group is not yet very high, you may want to try a more anonymous procedure the first time or two. After posting the two questions on the wall for the group, tell participants that you will be leaving the room for the next 10 minutes and you sincerely ask their honest evaluation of the meeting. Ask them to write down their individual responses to the two questions posed. Explain that they should not sign their names, but you would appreciate their specific suggestions and assessment. If participants are still writing their comments after 10 minutes, allow a few more minutes. When you return, express your appreciation to them and take the flip charts back to your worksite for careful analysis. (Don't be defensive!) Then be sure to follow up with meaningful changes in subsequent meetings!

THE HUMAN SPIDER WEB

OBJECTIVES

To warm up a team and break down their inhibitions.

To provide an opportunity for members to work as a team and explore the dimensions of teamwork.

To energize a team meeting.

MATERIALS REQUIRED

None.

PROCEDURE

This exercise works best with a small team. If you have a larger team, divide it into groups of 6–8 individuals. Have each group move to a location that allows them to stand in a small circle.

Instruct members of each group to extend their left hands across the circle and grasp the right hands of the other members who are approximately opposite them. Then have them extend their right hands across the circle and grasp the left hands of other individuals.

Inform them that their task is to unravel the spider web of interlocking arms without letting go of anyone's hands. If you have one team, inform them that they will be timed (as a way to place pressure on them); if you have several groups, tell them they will be competing with other groups to see who finishes the task first.

DISCUSSION QUESTIONS

1. What was your first thought when you heard the nature of the task? (Probably: "This will be impossible!")

2. What member behaviors detracted (or could detract) from the group's success in achieving its goal?

3. What lessons does this exercise have for future team building?

TIP

Solving this exercise depends on someone's capacity to see the whole picture, assume a leadership role, and communicate clearly. The key lies in having members step over another's arms to disentangle themselves until a circle is complete. Therefore, it is recommended that all team members be wearing suitable (i.e., casual) clothes.

PLENTIFUL PROVERBS PREACH POETICALLY

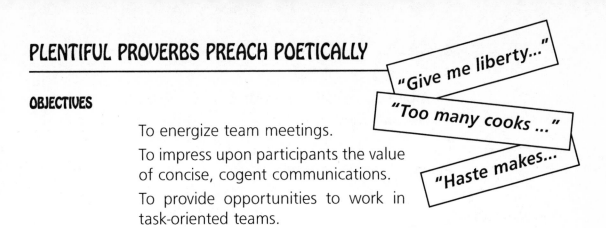

"Give me liberty..."

"Too many cooks ..."

"Haste makes..."

OBJECTIVES

To energize team meetings.

To impress upon participants the value of concise, cogent communications.

To provide opportunities to work in task-oriented teams.

MATERIALS REQUIRED

Sufficient copies of the Proverb Simplification Exercise for all team members.

PROCEDURE

Distribute copies of the exercise appearing on page 185 to all members.

Remind them that a proverb is defined as "a short, pithy saying in frequent and widespread use, expressing a well-known truth or fact."

Ask them to translate each hidden proverb into its more commonly known and poetic form. (This can be done individually or in groups.)

When sufficient time has been provided, randomly call on individuals to disclose their interpretations of what each proverb says. (This can provide a substantial opportunity for levity.)

Engage the group in a debriefing session, in which these answers are shared, and some or all of the discussion questions are used:

1. A fool and his or her money are soon parted.

2. When the cat's away, the mice will play.

3. Too many cooks spoil the broth.

4. Haste makes waste.
5. Crime does not pay.
6. A bird in the hand is worth two in the bush.
7. The early bird gets the worm.
8. Give me liberty or give me death.
9. Better late than never.

DISCUSSION QUESTIONS

1. Who talks or writes like this on our team? Why?
2. What is the impact of such obfuscation (Okay, we're guilty, too!) on effective communication?

TIP

If you note a large number of blank looks after a few minutes, it is wise to share one example with the group. This will illustrate what they are to accomplish.

PROVERB SIMPLIFICATION EXERCISE

DIRECTIONS: *Beneath each statement, write the more common hidden proverb that expresses the same meaning in simple language.*

1. An ignoramus and his or her lucre are readily disjoined.

2. In the absence of the feline race, certain small rodents will give themselves up to various pleasurable pastimes.

3. A plethora of culinary specialists vitiate the liquid in which a variety of nutritional substances have been simmered.

4. Impetuous celerity engenders purposeless spoilage.

5. Illegal transgression offers no remuneration for its perpetrators.

6. A winged and feathered animal in the digital limb is as valuable as a duet in the shrubbery.

7. The warm-blooded class aves who is governed by promptitude can apprehend the small, elongated, and slender creeping animal.

8. Provide the privilege of enfranchisement, or I will feel that life is not worth living.

9. A condition characterized by tardiness is more desirable than one that is systematically marked by eternal absenteeism.

10

What Lies Ahead?

Coping with Change

THE GREAT PRETENDER: LOOKING AT OLD ISSUES FROM A NEW PERSPECTIVE

OBJECTIVES

To help team members examine old issues from a new perspective.

To explore the validity of first impressions.

To stimulate creativity and thinking out-of-the-box.

MATERIALS REQUIRED

None.

PROCEDURE

At the start of a team meeting, explain to the members that they will have a chance to be someone else today. Once they decide who they want to be, they must keep that a secret during the meeting. As they make decisions or contributions to the meeting, they are to take the perspective of the person whose character they have assumed (e.g., a respected business leader, scientist, environmentalist, political figure, customer, supplier). If they decide to just be themselves, that is acceptable, but that, too, must remain a secret.

Toward the end of the meeting, have individuals introduce themselves by their real names, reveal the names of their characters, and state why they chose the characters they assumed.

DISCUSSION QUESTIONS

1. How did it feel being the Great Pretender?

2. Were you surprised to learn of others' identities?

3. What new perspectives on old problems did you gain?
4. How do first impressions affect our feelings toward others?
5. How did being someone else make you feel about yourself?
6. How did assuming someone else's persona affect your decisions, contributions to the meeting, and comfort level in sharing your views?

IF YOU HAVE MORE TIME

Once team members have decided who they want to be (allow a minute or two for this), break them into subgroups of 3–4 people. At this time, have each person introduce the character they are going to be. For the remainder of the day or meeting, members are to stay in these roles. For example, if they are millionaires, they might continually boast of their status, telling stories of their wealth and travels, etc.

MANAGING CHANGE

OBJECTIVE

To provide team members with an opportunity to analyze the change process and decide how to make future changes more readily palatable.

MATERIALS REQUIRED

None.

PROCEDURE

Identify a recent situation in which some type of change was introduced by your team. Provide a brief synopsis of that change and how it was initiated.

Hold a team discussion of the following questions:

1. Was the change resisted? Why or why not?
2. In retrospect, what could or should have been done to make the change easier? (Responses will usually center around such items as "better planning," "communication," "no surprises," etc.)

Note: Allow 10–15 minutes for group discussion. After the team has thoroughly reviewed the change, call on several members to report on their opinions, spending most of their oral report on question 2 above and the discussion questions below.

DISCUSSION QUESTIONS

1. What was done to add to the forces strengthening the proposed change?

2. What was done to weaken or remove the forces resisting the change?

3. At what stage did the tide turn in favor (or against!) the proposed change? Why?

TIP

Groups often remain focused on the details of a specific change. Encourage them to derive broader action principles that they can use to guide future change efforts more effectively.

THE 10 PERCENT STRETCH

OBJECTIVE

To impress upon team members that no matter how well they are performing now, they are probably capable of doing better.

MATERIALS REQUIRED

None.

PROCEDURE

Ask a volunteer to step to the side of the room. Request that the person extend an arm and reach as high on the wall as she or he can. Be prepared to have some way to assess approximately how high the person's outstretched fingertips reached.

Now ask them to extend an arm again and, by *really stretching,* reach as high on the wall as possible. Note how far the fingertips extended this time (it will invariably be farther).

Stress a few major points from this exercise (or, preferably, ask the team to derive its own conclusions from the demonstration). Ask them to note the effects of a 10 percent improvement by a baseball player, for example—more hits, more total bases, fewer errors.

DISCUSSION QUESTIONS

1. What apprehensions do we have about doing something new or different?
2. Could our team improve performance in some area by 10 percent or more? In what areas?

3. What message might we be sending to the organization and customers when we emphasize the value of a 10 percent improvement in performance at work?

4. In what ways have we learned to hold some portion of our energy or talent in reserve?

TIP

You may find that some persons will exhibit defensiveness by indicating that they are already working as hard as they can. Without debating their behavior, simply ask them if they are aware of any other employees who are not contributing all they possibly can. (They'll rarely deny this phenomenon!)

SOURCE

Richard L. Hughes, et al., *Leadership*, Homewood, Illinois: Irwin, 1993, pp. 37–39.

WHAT IF ...

OBJECTIVE

To provide an opportunity for group members to prepare contingency plans for potentially serious or disastrous situations.

MATERIALS REQUIRED

Sponge-type ball.

PROCEDURE

After a brief review of the rules of brainstorming (no criticism; quantity, not quality; etc.), tell the group they will now get some practice in handling future problems.

Ask the members to think of a recent situation they either experienced or observed that featured Murphy's Law (i.e., "If anything can possibly go wrong, it will.").

Form triads and have each trio agree on one potential real-world problem that could occur (e.g., What if the PA set didn't work? What if the sales brochures don't arrive on schedule? What if the computer crashes?).

Select one group to pose its problem orally and then throw the ball (gently!) to another group. Whoever catches it must offer some possible solutions. (If necessary, allow other participants to also offer viable answers.)

The solution-generating group then states its problem ("What if ...") and tosses the ball to another group, who offer possible solutions. Continue as time allows.

DISCUSSION QUESTIONS

1. What prevents us from seeing our own solutions?

2. Why is it we can "see" solutions to others' problems much more easily?

3. What implications does this exercise have for us at work?

TIP

Encourage the problem-presenting group to really listen and look for the merits in each solution received. Caution them not to fall into the trap of "yes-but" thinking.

11

How Can We Have More Fun?

Taking Time to Play

IF LIARS CAN FIGURE, CAN FIGURES LIE?

OBJECTIVE

To alert team members to the fact that they must always be alert to the possibility that what they hear may need to be questioned, examined, and challenged. This brainteaser is just for fun. Use it halfway through a long meeting to reenergize your team and practice creative thinking.

MATERIALS REQUIRED

Copies of A Simple Arithmetic Test.

PROCEDURE

Distribute copies of the test to the team members (alternatively, project a copy of it on an overhead transparency projector).

Create a sense of urgency by indicating that you will allow exactly 2 minutes for completion of the test. Ask participants not to disclose their choices until all team members have finished the test.

Ask the group for their responses (preferably, tabulate the number who underlined each of the seven problems on the chalkboard or on a prepared transparency).

Mention that there are 3 false assertions. If someone objects that there are only 2 items arithmetically incorrect (numbers 2 and 3 are false), point out that therefore the initial assertion is false. Consequently, that assertion becomes the third false statement that they were to identify. Reward the winner of this correct answer with a prize.

DISCUSSION QUESTIONS

1. Were the directions clear and unambiguous? If so, why were they misinterpreted?
2. What are the reasons facilitators' statements and assertions are often readily accepted, and almost naively believed?
3. Under what conditions should facilitators' assertions be less readily accepted and even challenged?

SOURCE

Adapted from Martin Gardner, *Aha Gotcha!*, San Francisco: W. H. Freeman & Co., 1982, p. 8.

A SIMPLE ARITHMETIC TEST

DIRECTIONS: *There are three false statements here. Identify them by underlining each one. Please work quickly. Raise your hand when you are done.*

1. $\sqrt{169} = 13$

2. $243 \div 3 = 61$

3. $4 \times 27 = 98$

4. $(213 - 23)/2 = 95$

5. $(7)^3 = 343$

6. $242 - 12/3 = 238$

7. $6^2 + 8^2 = \sqrt{10,000}$

SCRAMBLED CITIES

OBJECTIVE

This brainteaser is just for fun. Use it halfway through a long meeting to reenergize your team and practice creative thinking.

MATERIALS REQUIRED

Copies of the Scrambled Cities quiz.

PROCEDURE

Distribute copies of the Scrambled Cities quiz to each participant. Each item can be unscrambled to identify a city. Award an inexpensive prize to the first person who completes the quiz correctly. (The answers are provided on page 207.)

SCRAMBLED CITIES QUIZ

1. OIAPER　　　＿＿＿＿＿＿

2. REEDVN　　　＿＿＿＿＿＿

3. ITSUAN　　　＿＿＿＿＿＿

4. TEEATSL　　　＿＿＿＿＿＿

5. LE OASP　　　＿＿＿＿＿＿

6. LUULOONH　　　＿＿＿＿＿＿

7. WNE ALROESN　　　＿＿＿＿＿＿

8. SNA TANNOOI　　　＿＿＿＿＿＿

9. AKNSSA ITCY　　　＿＿＿＿＿＿

10. SOL SEELGNA　　　＿＿＿＿＿＿

11. SNA SEJO　　　＿＿＿＿＿＿

12. ULBOCKB　　　＿＿＿＿＿＿

13. ACHIWTI　　　＿＿＿＿＿＿

14. XNOIEPH　　　＿＿＿＿＿＿

15. AAPTM　　　＿＿＿＿＿＿

16. ULTAS　　　＿＿＿＿＿＿

17. GACOHIC　　　＿＿＿＿＿＿

18. NAS GOIDE　　　＿＿＿＿＿＿

19. THOUSNO　　　＿＿＿＿＿＿

20. PROTLDAN　　　＿＿＿＿＿＿

ANSWERS TO SCRAMBLED CITIES QUIZ

1. Peoria
2. Denver
3. Austin
4. Seattle
5. El Paso
6. Honolulu
7. New Orleans
8. San Antonio
9. Kansas City
10. Los Angeles
11. San Jose
12. Lubbock
13. Wichita
14. Phoenix
15. Tampa
16. Tulsa
17. Chicago
18. San Diego
19. Houston
20. Portland

BRAINTEASER I I.Q. TEST

OBJECTIVE

This brainteaser is just for fun. Use it halfway through a long meeting to reenergize your team and practice creative thinking.

MATERIALS REQUIRED

Handout sheets for each person or small group.

PROCEDURE

Hand out copies of the Brainteaser I I.Q. Test. Suggest that each block represents a well-known phrase or saying.

BRAINTEASER I I.Q. TEST

DIRECTIONS: *Here are some real puzzlers for you! Decipher the hidden meaning of each set of words.*

1	2	3	4
FGH ^I JKLMNOP ^Q RST	EILNPU	**PLASMA** H_2O	M O ^N O S I T E
5	**6**	**7**	**8**
NOXQQIVIT	**arrest you're**	RUINS RUINS RUINS RUINS RUINS LOVE RUINS RUINS RUINS	PICT ^U RES
9	**10**	**11**	**12**
L NCH L NCH	44444	***DISTANCE***	**P** **NOANO** **Y**
13	**14**	**15**	**16**
cy cy	**B ILL ED**	**POLMOMICE**	HIGH CLOUDS CLOUDS CLOUDS CLOUDS CLOUDS

211

BRAINTEASER I I.Q. TEST ANSWERS

1. High IQ
2. Line up
3. Blood is thicker than water
4. Mixed emotions
5. No excuse for it
6. You're under arrest
7. Love among the ruins
8. You ought to be in pictures
9. Take you out to lunch
10. Petits fours
11. Distance running
12. Pay through the nose
13. Cyclones
14. Sick in bed
15. Mother-in-law
16. High above the clouds

BRAINTEASER II I.Q. TEST

OBJECTIVE

This brainteaser is just for fun. Use it halfway through a long meeting to reenergize your team and practice creative thinking.

MATERIALS REQUIRED

Handout sheets for each person or small group.

PROCEDURE

Hand out copies of the Brainteaser II I.Q. Test. Suggest that each block represents a well-known phrase or saying.

BRAINTEASER II I.Q. TEST

DIRECTIONS: *Here are some real puzzlers for you! Decipher the hidden meaning of each set of words.*

1 **HAMLET WORDS**	2 d o o d l e	3 late n e v er	4 **c l o u**
5 **head** **lo ve** **heels**	6 **THAT**	7 **BED FA ST**	8 ◯ **ME**
9 CAR JACK TON	10 **1. GLANCE** **2.** **3. GLANCE**	11 momanon	12 **ca se** **case**
13 GINBEERVODKASHSHERRYRUM (in circle)	14 NIN1H	15 **c c c c** **HOLIDAY**	16 **SKI**_{**I**}**NG**

217

BRAINTEASER II I.Q. TEST ANSWERS

1. Play on words
2. Dipsy doodle
3. Better late than never
4. Partly cloudy
5. Head over heels in love
6. Fancy that
7. Bed and breakfast
8. This round is on me
9. Jack-in-the-box
10. Without a second glance
11. Man in the moon
12. Open-and-shut case
13. A round of drinks
14. Middle of the ninth
15. Overseas holiday
16. Downhill skiing

BRAINTEASER III I.Q. TEST

sitting
world

OBJECTIVE

This brainteaser is just for fun. Use it halfway through a long meeting to reenergize your team and practice creative thinking.

MATERIALS REQUIRED

Handout sheets for each person or small group.

PROCEDURE

Hand out copies of the Brainteaser III I.Q. Test. Suggest that each block represents a well-known phrase or saying.

BRAINTEASER III I.Q. TEST

DIRECTIONS: *Here are some real puzzlers for you! Decipher the hidden meaning of each set of words.*

1 cry m i l k	**2** **MAN** **campus**	**3** 111111 another another another another another another	**4** **BUSINES**
5 C A N C E L L E D	**6** ◯ ◯(MOVING) ◯ ◯(MOVING)	**7** **R O A D**	**8** sitting world
9 ME ME ME AL AL AL day	**10** VIT _ MIN	**11** S T E P P I N G	**12** **REVIRDTAES**
13 **NO NO** ――――――― **CORRECT**	**14** head ache	**15** heatheatheatheat	**16** M OUNTAIN

223

BRAINTEASER III I.Q. TEST ANSWERS

HANDOUT

1. Cry over spilled milk
2. Big man on campus
3. Six of one; half dozen of another
4. Unfinished business
5. Cancelled check
6. Moving in the right circles
7. Middle of the road
8. Sitting on top of the world
9. Three square meals a day
10. Vitamin A deficiency
11. Stepping over
12. Backseat driver
13. Right under your nose
14. Splitting headache
15. Heatwave
16. Mountain climbing

CONTENT REVIEW TRIVIA QUIZ

OBJECTIVES

To review key points in a presentation you've just made.

To test how well people are remembering what you've said.

MATERIALS REQUIRED

Printed handout or prepared transparency.

PROCEDURE

Following the presentation of new material on any topic, announce that you will now give a short quiz on the information covered. Distribute the prepared quiz, in which you have interspersed (e.g., odd/even) a set of outrageously trivial questions with a set of legitimate questions. Turn this activity into a competition or group activity to find the greatest number of correct answers in the given amount of time. Sample trivia questions include:

1. What is the length of a dollar bill (in centimeters)? (Answer: 15½)
2. How many matches are in a book? (Answer: 20)
3. At what temperature are Fahrenheit and Centigrade equal? (Answer: −40°)
4. What is a group of lions called? (Answer: Pride)
5. How many full moons are there in a year? (Answer: 13)
6. How do they put lead into a pencil? (Answer: they make two halves, insert the lead, and glue it together.)
7. What letter do the greatest number of words in the dictionary begin with? (Answer: S)

When all are completed, solicit sample answers to each question. Use this opportunity to review the main points of your presentation. Reward the person or group having the greatest number of correct answers with a prize.

SOURCE

Bill Allen, Nestle, Canada; Don Mills, Ontario.

12

How Can We Build Self-esteem?

Affirming Ourselves through Games

POSITIVE SELF-CONCEPT

OBJECTIVES

To demonstrate that it is acceptable for team members to be proud of themselves.

To stress that is is okay to express self-pride.

MATERIALS REQUIRED

None.

PROCEDURE

Have the team members divide themselves into pairs.

Ask everyone to write on a sheet of paper 4 or 5 things they really like about themselves.

After 3–4 minutes have passed, ask team members to share with their respective partners the items they wrote down.

Then have each person list several less desirable habits that they would like to change about themselves. Again, ask them to share these items with their respective partners.

DISCUSSION QUESTIONS

1. Did you feel uncomfortable with this activity? If so, why? (We've been culturally conditioned not to expose our egos to others, even if it is valid to do so.)
2. Were you honest with yourself, or did you hold back on your good traits? How about your bad traits?
3. What reactions (e.g., surprise, encouragement, reinforcement) did you get from your partner when you disclosed your strengths? Did the reactions differ when you disclosed your bad habits?

231

TIP

Since most people tend to be overly modest and hesitant to write something nice about themselves, some light encouragement on your part may be needed. For example, you may spontaneously disclose your list, such as "enthusiastic, honest, serious, intelligent, graceful."

PROVIDING POSITIVE FEEDBACK

OBJECTIVE

To encourage people to give positive strokes to others.

MATERIALS REQUIRED

None.

PROCEDURE

Note: This exercise may be used to follow the previous one, Positive Self-Concept (page 231).

Introduce the session by suggesting that we all need and crave recognition and positive strokes.

Divide the team into groups of two.

Ask each person to write 4–5 things they've noticed in their partner, such as:

✔ One physical feature that is particularly nice, e.g., a nice smile or pleasant voice.

✔ One personality trait that is unusually pleasant, e.g., considerate of others, patient, neat.

✔ One talent or skill that is noteworthy, e.g., a good public speaker, accurate typist.

The items must all be positive ones.

After a few minutes of writing, open discussion follows for each group of two, wherein the observer states what he or she wrote about the other.

Suggest that each person record his or her partner's positive feedback and save it to read on a "bummer" day.

DISCUSSION QUESTIONS

1. Were you comfortable with this exercise? If not, why? (It may be a new experience to be both giver and receiver of positive feedback.)

2. Why is it difficult for many of us to give another person a compliment?

3. What would make it easier for us to give positive feedback to others? (Develop a close relationship first; provide validating evidence; choose an appropriate time.)

4. What would make it easier for us to receive positive feedback from others? (Practice accepting it with grace; resolve to ponder its validity first before challenging it; allow yourself to feel good about it.)

5. Why is it that some people are quick to give a negative comment, but seldom, if ever, have anything nice to say about people?

TIP

This can be a powerful exercise, especially if participants have known each other for some time. A similar process is also known as a "strength bombardment," wherein you simply select one focal person to be the recipient at each (weekly) team meeting, and then have all other members share their positive assessments of that person.

SUGAR GRAM

OBJECTIVE

To acquaint people with their abilities to give and receive compliments. In minutes the effects are realized—and the team climate is enhanced.

> ## Sugar Gram
>
> You are ...
>
> You have ...
>
> You can ...

MATERIALS REQUIRED

Paper, pencils, or pens—and some honest giving.

PROCEDURE

Each individual is given approximately 5 minutes to write as many positive compliments (sugar grams) that are honest, to as many teammates as possible. They can be surface compliments (your tie is nice, your dress looks nice on you, etc.) or they can be more personal (whatever the sender feels comfortable giving). The only other criterion is that there must be eye contact when delivering the compliments. They can be anonymous and folded, but each person must look at the recipient when handing them out.

The recipients cannot open any sugar grams until everyone is finished handing them out. Then everyone sits down to unwrap their presents at the same time.

Comment on the general mood present, the nonverbal signals being sent out, the smiles.

Before giving members the signal to read their sugar grams, ask: "How many of you received at least one gram from someone you did not write one to?" "How did it make you feel?" Perhaps that is why so many of us disregard honest compliments—because we respond by just giving out another one, etc....

Everyone opens the grams and the mood is heightened even more. The supportive team climate will be apparent. Some members may be a bit embarrassed, but there will be no denying that the experience was pleasurable.

DISCUSSION QUESTIONS

1. Why do we hold back on honest compliments to those we care about, work with, or even observe?

2. How did you feel when reading what people wrote about you?

3. Could you adapt and use this practice as part of your style to become more aware—and more receptive?

4. Did the fact that the sugar grams were anonymous have any significance? Why? Would it be better if they were signed?

5. If you were to match up those with whom you had eye contact and the sugar grams you received, how would you do it? What does that add to that relationship?

6. Are there any additional sugar grams you would like to write? Why not do it on your own when the feeling strikes?

TIPS

This activity is great before a break or at the end of a session.

The team leader should prepare a few sugar grams for each person to be used in the event someone may not receive one.

COLLECTING POSITIVE STROKES

What Made Me Feel the Best

What Surprised (or Confused) Me Most

OBJECTIVE

To end a team meeting on a positive note.

MATERIALS REQUIRED

One large envelope and one set of 3 × 5 cards per member.

PROCEDURE

Provide each team member with one blank 3 × 5 card for every other member (and a roster of names if people don't know each other well). At the beginning of the meeting, instruct members to observe their teammates' behaviors closely, and write one positive remark about each person on a card. (The team leader may also choose to be a participant in this process—both as a contributor and as a recipient.)

Toward the end of the meeting, collect the cards (be sure the intended recipients' names are on them), sort them into the appropriate envelopes, and distribute them to each person. Allow adequate time to let each person scan quickly through the set. This allows all members to leave the meeting with some positive feelings about themselves, even though the meeting may have been stressful.

DISCUSSION QUESTIONS

1. If time permits, ask each member to read aloud the single card that made him or her feel the best.
2. Ask each member to read aloud the single card that surprised (or confused) him or her.

Ask each team member to provide each teammate with "One tip for your success."

Ask each team member to complete this sentence for each other member: "I wish you would ...."

TIP

This process can also be adapted to focus on the whole team (instead of individual members). Ask members to write down what they like about the team, or what went well today. Then collect and share the anonymous cards. Later, as the team gains comfort with the method, the process can become oral.

About the authors

Dr. John W. Newstrom is a university professor, noted author, and consultant to organizations in the areas of training and supervisory development. He is currently a professor of human resource management in the School of Business and Economics at the University of Minnesota, Duluth, where he teaches courses and workshops in the fields of organizational change, human resource development, management, and interpersonal and group relations. He has conducted training programs on a wide range of topics for organizations including 3M Co., Lakehead Pipeline, LTV Steel Mining, Blandin Paper Co., Diamond Tool, Minnesota Power, Clyde Iron, City of Scottsdale, Armour-Dial, and St. Luke's Hospital.

John has been active in the American Society for Training and Development (ASTD) since 1971 and has been a popular speaker, appearing before many ASTD chapters throughout the United States.

Dr. Newstrom has written ten articles for the *Training and Development Journal,* serves on the Editorial Review Board for the *Journal of Management Development,* and is the co-author (with Ed Scannell) of the widely acclaimed books *Games Trainers Play, More Games Trainers Play, Still More Games Trainers Play,* and *Even More Games Trainers Play.* He has also co-authored, in recent years:

- *The Manager's Bookshelf* (with Jon Pierce)
- *Organizational Behavior* (with Keith Davis)
- *Windows into Organizations* (with Jon Pierce)
- *What Every Supervisor Should Know* (with Lester Bittel)
- *Transfer of Training* (with Mary Broad)
- *Leaders and the Leadership Process* (with Jon Pierce)

An active member of the National Speakers Association, **Edward E. Scannell** has given more than one thousand presentations, seminars, and workshops across the United States and in several overseas venues.

Equally involved in both civic and professional organizations, he has served on the boards of directors of a number of groups, including the Tempe Chamber of Commerce, the American Society for Training and Development (ASTD), Meeting Professionals International (MPI), and the National Speakers Association. He was elected National President of ASTD in 1982 and later served a two-year term as the Executive Chairman of the International Federation of Training and Development Organizations.

He has written or co-authored several books and over one hundred articles in the fields of human resource management, communication, creativity, meeting planning, management, and teambuilding. His best-selling *Games Trainers Play* series (McGraw-Hill), co-authored with John W. Newstrom, is used by speakers, trainers, and meeting planners around the world.

Formerly the Director of the University Conference Bureau at Arizona State University, Mr. Scannell also taught at the ASU College of Business and at the University of Northern Iowa. He is currently serving as the Director of the Center for Professional Development and Training in Scottsdale, Arizona.